New Paths and Second Careers for Lawyers

GEORGE H. CAIN

Senior Lawyers Division

American Bar Association

Cover design by Seven Rays, Inc.

Printed in the United States of America.

Library of Congress Catalog Card Number 93-74998
ISBN 0-89707-959-0

99 98 97 96 95 5 4 3 2

CONTENTS

PREFACE

A second career is the ambition of many lawyers, young and old. This revelation comes through in comments you and I hear every day from friends and colleagues in the profession. Theirs is a gentle plea for help in finding a new way of life.

Several years ago, after I became Chair of the Committee on Second Careers of the Senior Lawyers Division of the American Bar Association, I developed a deeper interest in career-change problems and their solutions. I contacted lawyers who had significant achievements in more than one career, and many responded to my requests for their prescriptions for success. This book presents some of their stories.

Knowing that so many fellow lawyers were seeking help led me to write this book. Some of the information I have assembled was graciously supplied by other people, and some suggestions are based on my experience in forty-five years of law practice.

I hope that the analysis of problems you may face, and our suggestions for their resolution, will prove helpful to you as you explore options for your second career.

George H. Cain
Riverside, Connecticut

ACKNOWLEDGMENTS

This book could not have been completed without the dedicated assistance of many people.

There are those who helped to outline its content and provided much editorial assistance and support: Victor Futter, who was Chair of the Publications Committee of the Senior Lawyers Division of the ABA, which undertook this project; Donald J. Gecewicz of ABA Publications Planning & Marketing, who shepherded the book from manuscript to final binding; Judge Glenn Robert Lawrence, who worked with Dr. Isaiah M. Zimmerman to explain some of the personal issues involved in a career change; E. Nobles Lowe, Chair of the Book Subcommittee of the Senior Lawyers Division, who made sure that contributors of essential data were available; Harlan Pomeroy, who took valuable time from his work with the Central and Eastern European Law Initiative in Bulgaria to make a valuable contribution to the chapter on community service; Professor Julius J. Marke, Jr., of the St. John's University Law School Library, who contributed to the discussion of law librarianship; and Dr. Lawrence R. Richard, who, while completing his doctoral dissertation, found time to write a section on the psychological problems involved in a career change; Harold A. Feder, Esq., of the Colorado bar, who assisted with the presentation on opportunities as an expert witness; Stanley B. Balbach, Esq., of the Illinois bar, who provided thoughtful suggestions on offering real estate counsel to seniors; and Scott B. Moser, Esq., of the Connecticut bar, and Robert Coulson, President of the American Arbitration Association, who made valuable contributions of materials for the discussion of alternative dispute resolution.

We are most appreciative to executives of the insurance industry who took time to provide detailed information on the factors and figures involved in calculating a malpractice insurance premium: Steven G. Brady of St. Paul F&M Insurance Co., Paul F. Mahaffey of Professional Liability Underwriting Managers, Inc., and Robert W. Minto, Jr., of Attorneys Liability Protective Society.

Many lawyers throughout the country and abroad responded to our requests for details as to the circumstances surrounding their decisions to embark upon second careers and the results of those decisions. The lives of some of these attorneys are profiled in the pages that follow. We thank Jean Allard of Illinois, Newton P. Allen of Tennessee, Charlotte P. Armstrong of New York, Terence H. Benbow of Connecticut, the late John C. Carter of Tennessee, Milo G. Coerper of the District of Columbia, Hon. Dorothea E. Donaldson of Florida, Amb. Edward R. Finch, Jr., of New York, Hon. James D. Hopkins of New York, Hon. Thomas J. Meskill of Connecticut, Hon. John D. Ong of Ohio, Donald E. Pease of Delaware, John E. Robson of Georgia, Isaac D. Russell of the U.S. Foreign Service (Ethiopia), M. J. Schmidt of Wisconsin, Darwin E. Smith of Texas, David Williamson Smith of New York, Jack Donald Voss of Ohio, Sydney A. Woodd-Cahusac of Connecticut, and Harold G. Wren of Kentucky.

Probably most important are those who took the time to read the manuscript and offer comments as we went along: Richard B. Allen of Illinois, David A. Bridewell of Illinois, Paul J. Cain of Ohio, Mary Collins of Connecticut, William E. Huth of Connecticut, Arthur W. Machen, Jr., of Maryland, Hon. Mary S. Parker of California, and Lester M. Ponder of Indiana.

Finally, there is my strongest critic, but ardent admirer, who gave time and careful thought to the words and ideas I produced. Without the encouragement and assistance of the light of my life, my wife, Connie, this task would never have been done.

Thanks to you all.

George H. Cain
Riverside, Connecticut

1

A Momentous Decision

Many lawyers, young and old, are opting for a second career. In the January–February 1992 issue of *Harvard Magazine,* Glenn Kaye, himself a Harvard Law School alumnus turned writer, discusses reasons why many relatively recent law school graduates have forsaken law as a career and turned elsewhere—or, if they have not made a switch, have a strong desire for change. *Experience,* the journal of the Senior Lawyers Division of the American Bar Association, has devoted more than one issue to discussing the career changes made late in life by older members of the bar.

What prompts lawyers, men and women, young and old, to contemplate a change in careers? The discussion in this and the following chapters will try to answer that question. We hope it will help you if you, too, are wondering about a second career.

The Baby Boomers

Younger lawyers, raised as baby boomers and accustomed to a much more relaxed life-style than their parents, in many cases find the life of a lawyer too demanding of time, too devoid of opportunity for self-fulfillment, and too lacking in intellectual stimulation. While the earnings of some young lawyers may outdistance the earnings of their contemporaries in other professions, the time constraints of law practice prohibit using the extra cash for such things as visits to the opera, the ballet, or a professional ball game. There doesn't even seem to be time to read a book or take the kids to the park.

In major law firms, the requirement that younger lawyers spend days and weeks dedicated to one specific aspect of a single case conflicts with the lawyer's desire to see something accomplished—and quickly. The monotony of life in law practice, for lawyers in smaller firms who may deal constantly with repetitive situations as well as for their brethren in the larger "law factories," brings some to the conclusion that the only answer is a second career.

Then, as Mr. Kaye's article points out, some young people find that they are just not temperamentally suited to the law, which by its nature is confrontational, combative, and adversarial. Some people would simply rather "switch than fight." The daily challenge to find a solution that will better their opponent is upsetting to this group of lawyers, and they elect to find a second career more in tune with their thinking.

Age and Experience

The desire for a second career is not confined to young people. Many experienced lawyers, some in middle age and others approaching retirement, also seek change. While some may consider their careers unsatisfying or even distasteful, more often their reason runs deeper: the desire to contribute to society in a different or more meaningful way. For example, we know of lawyers with successful practices who have elected to join the United States Foreign Service, thereby enhancing their own life experience as well as contributing to their country through foreign service. Others have elected to attend a seminary and join the clergy to assist others in the spiritual realm.

If you want to read some of the horror stories of attorneys who became disenchanted with the law and decided to embark upon other careers, try Deborah L. Arron's book *Running from the Law*, originally published by Ten Speed Press in 1989. Should you believe that the practice of law—in whatever form—is interesting and challenging, albeit demanding, then you will probably conclude that most of the people who tell their stories in Ms. Arron's book should never have become lawyers in the first place.

Lawyers approaching retirement age have some of the same reasons for choosing a second career as do younger lawyers, but their age adds an extra dimension. A person who is sound of mind and body and yet is forced to retire may want to keep active and interested in life; a new, different second career seems an obvious choice. If that person needs some additional income to supplement whatever pension is available, a second career that will offer compensation after retirement may not only be desirable but necessary.

To decide what second careers may be feasible in a given situation, it is helpful to consider all of the various factors that affect the choice. Although this book is devoted in the main to discussions of the life for lawyers after retirement, and thus relates primarily to the older lawyer, the factors one must consider as a senior should also be on the checklist of the junior lawyer who is contemplating a career change.

Thinking about Your Options

The approach to a second career involves different considerations for the person about to retire and for the person who is merely unhappy with his or her present position.

Let us first talk a little more about the person about to retire. It is well understood that retirement is a traumatic experience for most active people. Consequently, you should consider it well ahead of its happening, evaluate the opportunities it presents—for work and for play—and decide your best course. Later in this volume you will find a discussion of the need for personal self-appraisal, the necessity to look at your own financial resources and decide how they relate to any future activity you might wish to pursue, and the psychological effect that your retirement will have on your spouse, your children, and your associates.

It is sufficient at this point to state that as retirement approaches, it is necessary to think about how your future life is to be spent. Some people are workaholics who *never* want to retire from very active work. Others are content to do absolutely nothing resembling work; they may look forward to constantly improving a golf or tennis game, or to sailing, travel, or just loafing. In between are those who want a little of all of the above. Whether you choose to carry a heavy work load or to work just enough to keep life interesting, it is important to start early to plan how to reach the desired level. Some firms permit retired partners to continue to represent a few clients; others condition the continued association with the firm on the retiree's agreement not to practice law, although allowing him or her to carry on other law-related activities, such as arbitration or mediation, marketing and client development, public speaking, and so on. You must have a clear understanding with your law firm on this point. As suggested later in this volume, when negotiating an of counsel agreement, you should clearly define your understanding with the firm, in writing, and the issue of the extent and manner of your law practice must be covered in that written agreement.

Many of the considerations as to whether a second career is desirable or feasible for the older lawyer about to retire apply equally to the younger or middle-aged lawyer seeking new frontiers.

How to Find a Second-Career Position

First, anyone who wants to seek a second career must do a thorough job of self-appraisal. In the tough, highly competitive economy today, every qualified person must go up against others who are also highly skilled. If you seek a career in the international area, for example, you need to consider your abilities with foreign languages and whether any existing health problems might make service abroad difficult. Also, there are angles to be covered in your resume. You need to review your networking skills. Have you alerted your alma mater(s)? Have you thought about how to handle yourself in an interview? Where are the sources in your search for a second career? These issues are discussed in some detail in Chapter 2.

Then there is the question of financial resources. Lawyers are generally well compensated, and they become accustomed to incomes above the level of society in general. The lawyer who embarks upon a second career must decide whether it will provide sufficient income for the family to live at its expected level and, if not, whether there are other assets that will fill the gap. You need to evaluate your assets and your liabilities. Are you prepared for the costs of malpractice insurance? What are those costs? Have you any idea of the cost of running an office? What is the tax effect of your required withdrawals from your retirement plans? Resources and requirements in second-career efforts, including most of these matters, are discussed in Chapter 3. (The costs of setting up an office are reviewed in Chapter 5.)

The psychological problems involved in attempting a second career must also be addressed. A second career, particularly if it involves getting out of law practice entirely, can have effects on family, friends, and business associates. Since the new career may change the way others view you, the effect is personal. Are you a "rainmaker"? Do you want to continue to be one, or would you prefer doing something more altruistic? How do you make a psychological assessment and determine whether—or what—career change is right for you? How can you determine whether there is a psychological problem? And if so, how should it be evaluated and solved? These questions are discussed by two eminent psychologists, Drs. Isaiah Zimmerman and Lawrence R. Richard, in Chapter 4.

Various Choices in a Second Career

Many lawyers never want to leave the law; they only want a "change of scenery." How a second career is defined depends upon one's outlook. For the lawyer who reaches retirement age but elects to remain with his or her firm, the changed circumstances—no longer being a partner—bring new problems. In a sense, this is a change of career. There are questions in choosing between remaining with your firm and leaving, between moving from a large firm to a small firm, or vice versa. Then there is the possibility of setting up your own office, either alone or with others. What are the costs of doing that, in terms of both capital investment and operating expense? What must you charge in order to cover those costs and provide an income for yourself? If you retire and choose either to remain with your present firm or to move to another law firm, what will the firm allow you to do? Where? How will you be compensated? Many of the various factors involved in assessing these choices are considered in Chapter 5.

Once you make a tentative choice, it is desirable to spell out the new status in a written agreement. In the course of considering what should be covered in that agreement, numerous other issues will be presented and will aid in making a final decision. These matters are discussed in Chapter 6, which considers the issues involved in negotiating an agreement.

Some people would say that the lawyer who makes a change from one law firm to another is not embarking upon a second career. That may be true if the lawyer has not yet reached retirement age and is therefore still a very active practitioner; but it is not so if he or she is a retiree. The lawyer who has retired from a law firm and decides to continue to practice with another firm or as a single practitioner believes, indeed, that it is a new and second career.

If the shift is from law practice to any field outside the law, then all would agree that the lawyer has *truly* embarked upon a second career.

What are some of the possibilities? Because of the lawyer's broad training and experience, the opportunities to move into many diverse areas are great. The life stories of many successful people reflect their beginnings as legal practitioners and their later shift into areas of work that benefited from their legal background. Many lawyers have moved from private practice into corporate law departments, into the judiciary, and into academia; others have shifted in the reverse direction. Some lawyers have opted for a life of politics and have devoted themselves to government service after a period of private practice. Judges and law professors have gone in the opposite direction, returning to private practice in order to increase their income and better provide for their families. In this book, we consider a variety of options available to any lawyer seeking a second career with compensation, and discuss them in some detail in Chapters 7 and 8.

Other paths a lawyer may follow are only quasi-legal in nature: A lawyer's background and experience are helpful, even necessary, but the work itself is not truly lawyer's work. The burgeoning field of alternative dispute resolution—with its many-faceted approach of mediation, fact finding, minitrials, and arbitration—is one example. Lawyers also are called upon to serve as expert witnesses in those fields of knowledge in which they are particularly competent: the law of their home state, when that happens to be the foreign law with regard to a case on trial; whether a fellow lawyer's conduct met the standards of the profession; and so on. Both of these choices for a second career are discussed in Chapter 9.

Finally, many lawyers with long service before the bar believe that upon retirement, it is time to give something back to their communities and to the world. These lawyers opt to use their legal experience in pro bono work, oftentimes as counsel to charitable or religious agencies that need assistance. As the Cold War has ended, countries in eastern Europe have found a need for guidance in formulating laws and regulations associated with democracy and free enterprise; many lawyers have volunteered to provide this counseling. These options are discussed in Chapter 10.

Considering this plethora of opportunity, some lawyers may wonder how such shifts of career are made. This book provides biographical sketches and some commentary from attorneys who have successfully moved into second careers. Their experiences prove that it can be done and show how to accomplish it.

Making Your Move

You will have to consider various alternatives, ranging from continuing to practice law, albeit in some different manner from your present regime, to abandoning the law altogether. In between, there are opportunities to combine the law with other activities. There are also choices between serving the world in a pro bono capacity and seeking substantial compensation for your efforts.

One tactic to follow is to sit down and write out on paper your own career history, including your accomplishments and failures, and base your future course on your own analysis of your past. As has been said, the past is prologue.

Nonetheless, the past is also experience. You must profit from it. You have learned what pleased you most in the past, and these past experiences should point you in the direction you wish to travel in the future. Many people rush headlong into career changes for which they are unsuited and for which they lack the necessary resources, whether those resources are intellectual, psychological, or financial. By noting some of the factors discussed in the chapters that follow and applying them to your own situation, you will be able to make a better choice of a second career. Should your choice require you to leave your present affiliation and find another, then you must find the organization or person needing your services and willing to take you on. If you have been with the same corporation or law firm, or with the same institution or government agency for a number of years, you have probably forgotten how to go about getting a job. In this book we also offer some suggestions as to how you might approach this aspect of the task.

Lawyers are a different breed. What is an appropriate path for other professions may not be appropriate for lawyers. We will try to make sure that you approach the question of a second career only after having considered all of the factors involved, when you are aware of the many opportunities open to you and can reach a sound decision.

2

Finding Your Opportunity

Let us assume you have decided you want a second career. You have examined the alternatives, consulted with your family and, where appropriate, with your business associates. And you have reviewed the financial considerations. Now you have come to the conclusion that it is time to act. What do you need to do to find that second career?

In this chapter, we will try to point you in the right direction and give you a few hints about the job search and how you might find a spot for yourself.

Although you will find thousands of jobs advertised in the national print media—the *New York Times*, the *Wall Street Journal*, *USA Today*, and so forth—most people with experience in employment placement will tell you that nothing beats networking when you are searching for a job. What is most effective in finding a job in a first career will also prove the most productive in finding a job in a second career. This is not to say that you should not follow up and respond to any opportunity presenting itself in the media, but because of the number of responses received by those placing the advertisements, you may have a better chance of winning your state lottery than finding a position by answering an ad. If you do respond to an advertisement in a newspaper or magazine, make sure you follow its instructions explicitly. Employers have good reason for requesting replies in a certain manner and format. Lawyers, particularly, are not supposed to behave in an unconventional fashion. Eccentricity will get you nowhere.

NETWORKING

Networking, stated simply, means that you let everyone you know be aware that you are seeking a second career—and what you have in mind doing. If you explain your plan to a friend, even if that friend has no possible chance, personally, of helping you, he or she may pass the information on to another person who is in exactly the position to be helpful.

Who should you make aware of your plans?

Start first with the people who know you and your abilities the best. Spread the word among your business associates: fellow lawyers in your firm, clients, lawyers who have been opponents in litigation or on the other side of transactions in which you were involved. You may also have had prior business relationships; people in these organizations who know and admire you are also candidates for your networking effort.

Next, make sure that your fellow alumni and alumnae are informed of your plans. Depending upon how you have maintained relationships over the years, you might go all the way back to high-school days. In most cases, the people likely to provide the most help are college and law school classmates.

Then there are the other members of the professional associations to which you belong, committee members with whom you have served, club members, church parishioners, and so on. Perhaps you have a sport or a hobby that interests you and there are others with whom you share your fun; make them aware of your career plan. It may be that your doctor or your dentist belongs to one or more organizations and may hear of an opportunity. Every one of these people associates with his or her own group of friends and professional contacts every day. They hear what is going on in the world and know when and where there is a need for help. They can pass along the information that you are available, capable, and interested in being of assistance.

Many people make the mistake of assuming that the only useful contacts are those with persons who can help them directly. Overlooked is the fact that every one of their friends and acquaintances knows many other people. When you make contacts in your network and let these people know that you are seeking a second career, ask them to pass the word to their network. In this way, you can let the world know that you are interested, available, and competent.

In the course of writing this book, I received a very interesting article written by Michael Adams for *Successful Meetings Magazine*. It appeared in the April 1991 issue and was sent to me by Belinda Plutz of Career Mentors, Inc., in New York. Ms. Plutz and Mr. Adams have similar views on the art of networking. He points out that networking is not merely employing the contacts you presently have, but constantly developing and expanding your sphere of interest. Nor is networking limited to specific situations. Networking is as possible and can be as productive on a commuter train as in a cocktail party at a fashionable resort.

Many people find it difficult to use the skills they need for successful networking. It is not easy for many people to enter a room of strangers and engage someone in conversation. Yet, this is the beginning of a successful network. As these experts tell us, always project genuine interest in people you meet and what they do; or as Michael Adams expresses it, "Be other-involved, not self-involved."

I have picked up a few pointers in my career and will pass them on to you. For instance, when you attend a convention or meeting where name tags are used, wear your tag on the right side, *not* the left; this allows your name to be plainly visible as you shake hands with a person you are meeting for the first time. It is also a help to someone who may not have seen you in a while, and who may remember your face but not your name. And when you meet someone in a large gathering (unless it is a person who knows you well), repeat your name as you extend your hand in greeting. This will assure that the person knows who you are; then, if you have a conversation about your second-career plans and you have occasion to contact this person, your name will be recognized.

Sometimes it happens that you are the bashful type and your spouse is more the extrovert. Should that be the case in your family, make the most of it. Your spouse can strike up the conversation that may widen your network and help you in your quest for a second career.

If someone gives you the name of a person to contact and you make the call, be sure to follow up with the person who assisted you by providing information on what happened. Showing your appreciation to those who help can only enhance the networking process.

There is no "best way" to contact these sources of help; you will have to judge how you can be most effective. Some people will respond to a letter, others to a telephone call, and still others to a visit. In any event, don't stop with one contact. Follow-up is important. Keep a record of the time and date of your contacts, and call or write again on an established schedule.

The Resume

Even if you are seeking a pro bono position as a second career, and certainly if you are looking for compensation, you will need a resume. Although it may have been many years since you have written one, you have probably read many resumes of other people in the course of your own work, and you know what impressed you and what did not.

As with many other pieces of writing, it is usually most effective to provide at the outset highlights of your life (birthplace, education, principal positions held) and your second-career objective. You can then embellish the job descriptions with details of your accomplishments in each assignment.

When it comes to this embellishment, I would disregard the advice of those who urge brevity. Brevity for its own sake is no virtue. Use as much space, put down as many words, as required to properly describe what you have done. If your life has been full of variety, then it obviously will take more space to outline what you have accomplished.

In this business of networking and being interviewed, rapport is almost as important as your educational and business credentials. People are drawn to other people with the same affiliations, the same interests in life. Consequently, your resume should not omit civic or military service, professional organizations to which you belong or have belonged, hobbies and sports that interest you, and decorations and awards that may have come your way.

Credentials

If you are a senior lawyer, known in your community, it may come as a shock that it may be necessary to produce *proof* that you did graduate from Siwash U. and that Briefcase Law School granted you a degree. In most cases, employers can verify your admission to the bar by a telephone call, and that in turn establishes your compliance with the state's educational requirements for bar admission. For the rare situation when that is insufficient proof or the employer is a cautious skeptic, make certain that your college and your law school are prepared to certify your graduation if requested.

Being Interviewed

It has probably been many years since you were the target of an employment interview. In the years that have intervened, you were the person who did the interviewing. Now it is time to stop and think about what you should do as the tables are reversed and you will be interviewed for a second-career position.

As soon as a time and date are established for an interview, get to work and research the background of the organization and people with whom you will be meeting. A visit to your local library will be well worth the effort. Find out exactly what the organization does and where it does it. Learn who the directors and officers are and where the offices are located. Try to make some inquiries and determine how decisions are made and who makes them. Discreet questioning of your friends who may have contacts with the organization may alert you to any particular policies that you should be familiar with. This information will help you conduct yourself well at the interview and will keep you from making any embarrassing mistakes.

Be yourself. Above all, you should be articulate but stick to the relevant points in the conversation.

Make a record of each interview, including the time, date, and place, as well as the names and positions of the people you met. You will find this useful in avoiding disconcerting situations down the road, should you communicate with an organization again.

WHERE TO FIND OPPORTUNITY

The appendix to this book provides a list of organizations you might contact in your search for a second career. But it is worthwhile to mention here a few other places where you might find that opportunity you seek.

Should you wish to contribute your services pro bono, you should contact the local office of the United Way in your area. Someone there may be aware of opportunities with member organizations. You might also contact the National Volunteer Center (at the address or phone number in the Appendix) for the names of other organizations seeking pro bono help. Bar associations in your area will most certainly have the names of organizations (and their contact persons) that need lawyers to provide pro bono legal service.

Tax lawyers may also contact the Internal Revenue Service in their region, as the IRS is seeking volunteer help in the tax season to answer taxpayers' questions. The firm of H&R Block also needs temporary help during the tax season; a visit or call to the local manager may be a fruitful activity.

Roman Catholic lawyers interested in working in the church as permanent deacons should speak with their pastors or the diocesan office concerning the training necessary for ordination, the time commitment required, and the compensation, if any, available in the diocese for this work.

BOOKS ON SECOND CAREERS

Your local library will have a number of reference books on second careers. Consulting these may provide some ideas as to what you might do and how you might do it, if you are determined to abandon your present career. Suffice it to mention here four:

Second Careers: New Ways to Work after 50, by Caroline Bird; Little, Brown & Co., 1992 (Appendix C, "Resources").

How to Change Your Career, by Kent Banning and Ardelle Friday; VGM Career Horizons, 1991.

The Whole Career Sourcebook, by Robbie Miller Kaplan; American Management Association, 1991.

Midstream Changes, by Nathan Anseng; Lerner Publications Company, 1990.

For those who are called to serve in a pro bono capacity, an excellent source of information on "how and where to find the best places to volunteer your time, [or] share your skills" is Judy Knipe's *Stand Up and Be Counted: The Volunteer Resource Book,* published by Simon & Schuster in 1992. Its several hundred pages list organizations classified by type. One can find opportunities for volunteering in the arts, in business, in community service, and the environment, to name just a few of the different groups covered in Ms. Knipe's work.

How One Lawyer Found a Second Career

People arrive at second-career decisions and find their niche in various ways.

What prompts a high-powered international lawyer—many times in the exciting forefront of significant developments, friendly with the lions of the profession, at the pinnacle of success—to contemplate a second career as a clergyman?

Milo G. Coerper was a quiet midwesterner from Milwaukee when he entered the Naval Academy at Annapolis in 1943. Graduated in 1946 along with Jimmy Carter and Stansfield Turner, he served his sea duty on the battleship *Iowa*. Then he went on to University of Michigan Law School, but was recalled to the Navy during the Korean conflict. After war service, he went back to University of Michigan Law School. There Milo developed an interest in international law, was graduated in 1954, and commenced law practice at Wilmer & Broun in Washington, D.C.

Milo's interest in international law led him to further study and receipt of M.A. and Ph.D. degrees from Georgetown University. In 1961, with this academic background, he joined the international firm of Coudert Bros. in its Washington office. At Coudert Bros., he worked with such giants of international practice as George Nebolsine, Percy Shay, Charles Torem, and Alexis Coudert. Later, Milo would work with Sol Linowitz and Louis Auchincloss. His ventures included involvement in such significant matters as defense of a case brought by Consumers Union against the federal government and American, Japanese, British, and German steelmakers for violation of U.S. antitrust laws. And he was the only non-European present in Luxembourg when the dignitaries of Europe met to welcome the British steel industry into the Common Market.

But even as his life brought him the excitement of history-making events, Milo was moving on a path that would broaden his spectrum still further. As he says:

> I began more and more to reflect not only on my life, but on "life" in general, and was drawn to delve more into philosophy, psychology, and spirituality. In doing so, I came upon Alexis Carrel's *Man, the Unknown*, first published in 1935, which Will Durant had referred to as "the wisest, profoundest, most valuable book that I have come upon in the American literature of our century." On the frontispiece I read, "To my Friends, Frederic R. Coudert, Cornelius Clifford, and Boris A. Bakhmeteff this book is dedicated." Later I found *The Voyage to Lourdes*, Alexis Carrel, 1950, with a preface by Charles A. Lindbergh, which stated in speaking of Carrel, "In New York, one was likely to find him in philosophical discussion with his three closest American friends—the head of a law firm, an ex-Russian Ambassador, and a Catholic priest." And, yes, my mentor, partner, and friend, Alexis Carrel Coudert, had been named after Alexis' father's close friend. . . .
>
> And, of course, I was reading Jung and learning about the "collective unconscious" and the feminine and masculine sides of the brain and Maslow and his "transcendental psychology" and "peak experiences." I was also delving into English spirituality, reading Julian of Norwich's *Revelations of Divine Love* and Evelyn Underhill's *Mysticism* and *The Mystics of the Church* and that led me to reading the Desert Fathers and Mothers, *The Rule of St. Benedict* (the father of Western Monasticism) and Thomas Merton. . . .
>
> At about this time in the mid-1970's, it came to me that we in the West pamper the body, exalt the intellect, and ignore the spirit. . . .
>
> I also was enlightened by Terry Holmes' two modes of consciousness—the *receptive* mode and the *action* mode (these relate to Jung's feminine and masculine psychological concepts). It's not all that simple, but these concepts are helpful. Most of us in the West live most of the time in the action mode—a mode of logic, control,

> analysis, and prediction—the mode of science and technology—and of the "warrior" and lawyer. The receptive mode is one of association, surrender, intuition, "surprise"—the mode of the artist, poet, and contemplative. To be a truly whole person we need to find some balance in our lives by at least "tasting" both modes.

All of this reading and contemplation had its effect on Milo. He and his wife had long ago acquired a home in the Maryland countryside and on Sundays attended an Episcopal church nearby. As Milo tells the story:

> One Sunday in May 1975 (on Pentecost—the birthday of the Church), while attending our little church in the country, I noticed that a silent, classical retreat on the Benedictine model was to be held at nearby St. James School and led by a Church of England priest who had just returned from India. Somehow I was drawn to take this on—it would test my monkish tendencies in a familiar and comfortable environment. It ran from a Tuesday afternoon through a Friday morning with structured worship, silence, and contemplative meditations. This was a most validating spiritual experience for me. I recalled Thomas Merton's statement on the purpose of the contemplative life: "to transform human consciousness through spirit and discipline." My consciousness had been transformed. I had "seen." What was the meaning of this for my life?
>
> I was not interested in changing my life. I loved my law firm, its tradition and reputation, and I liked my clients. Shortly thereafter I heard that a new four-year theological extension course created by the University of the South at Sewanee was to be given in the evenings at the College of Preachers at the Washington National Cathedral. I signed up.

Opportunity knocked at once for Milo Coerper. His country church was looking for an additional priest, one of two. The priests were not to be paid and were to keep their secular occupations. They would serve only on weekends, with other persons undertaking the administrative tasks of the parish. The congregation asked Milo if he would be willing to be one of their priests. Milo observes:

> The following Sunday during the Bishop's visitation, I was about to tell the congregation I did not feel worthy of their trust in me,

> when, before I knew it, one of the little old ladies (who has been trying to make a priest out of me ever since) took me up to the Bishop and introduced me as the second person they had selected to be trained as their priest. Well, that was it—and the beginning of a very rich ten years serving St. Andrew's.

After Fr. Milo Coerper retired as a curate at St. Andrew's in 1985, he commenced participation in a new program initiated at the Washington National Cathedral called the Navy Clergy Program. He officiates at services and counsels visitors on weekends, while his wife serves as a cathedral aide and leader of tours. Meanwhile, he continues as the oldest active partner of Coudert Bros.

Go to the Mountain

One thing to remember is that you must be aggressive and *seek out* your second-career opportunity. It is not likely to come looking for you. Don't wait. Once you have decided you want a second career, develop a plan and stick with it. Reviewing the lives of the men and women mentioned in the sidebars throughout this book, it is apparent that they did not give up the quest. They succeeded because they were diligent.

To quote again from Milo Coerper:

> Another point to be considered is whether you actually want to make a career change or whether you just want to add another dimension to your life. It may be frowned on in this modern world, but there are still a few renaissance people around who have more than one career at the same time. This may require some discernment, and give and take, but it can be done. Then there are those who are happily retired, but feel guilty because they aren't *doing* something. To these I would say, "Try emphasizing *being* rather than doing and you may find you'll be utilized. . . .
>
> In closing let me quote once again from Louis Auchincloss' autobiography and pass on a bit of "tough love": " . . . a man can spend his whole existence never learning the simple lesson that he has only one life and that if he fails to do what he wants with it, nobody else really cares."

As we can see from Milo Coerper's experience, a number of reasons led him to a second-career decision. Each of us may have some of these reasons, or different ones, for contemplating a career change. Whatever the reasons, there are factors in all of our lives that need to be considered before we are ready to employ the strategies discussed above. Two of these factors will be discussed in the chapters that follow: financial issues and psychological matters.

3

Financial Considerations

When you're about to decide whether or not to retire, regardless of your age, the frightening question arises: Can I afford it? The answer depends, of course, on what you plan to do. Certain second careers require more funds to get started than others, and some may actually generate more income than your first career.

Taking Inventory

The first step is to take inventory of your resources from the viewpoint of both available capital and anticipated income. What is the size of your personal investment portfolio? How much income will it produce? What is the amount of any pension that you may receive? What will you draw in Social Security payments? How much will you have to pay in federal and state income taxes? Remember, you will have to commence withdrawing from your Keogh and IRA accounts in the year after you reach age seventy and a half. (See the discussion on taxes later in this chapter.) Don't be fooled: While you are required to take money from these accounts and pay income taxes on the amount withdrawn, it is not really *income* to you; it represents your capital, and if you spend it, that amount is no longer producing income.

Next, determine how much you will need to keep yourself and your family in the style you feel you want to maintain. (Only a few people are able to retire without reducing their life-style to some extent.) Your capital is extremely important in your planning. You may elect to use some of it each year to provide funds for living expenses. Or you may decide to use it to borrow money, particularly if you decide on a second career that requires some capital investment. Your capital can thus provide security for a loan, should borrowing be necessary.

However, before deciding to commit capital for credit purposes, you must take stock of the expenditures necessary to maintain whatever standard of living you expect in retirement. Conventional wisdom has it that a person, particularly a professional, needs about 60 percent of preretirement income during retirement in order to maintain a comfortable life-style. What remains after the last dollar is derived from income and the last penny squeezed out of expenses can be used for debt service, if borrowing is necessary.

You complete your financial exercise; you determine how much income you will have available and how much you need. But there is a gap: The need exceeds the amount available. You now begin to think in terms of a second career, but one that will *produce income*. You cannot afford to work on a pro bono basis.

In deciding what sort of activity to pursue as a second career, you should also consider the costs associated with the various alternatives.

The Cost of Malpractice Insurance

One of the most significant expenditures for the lawyer who provides legal advice, whether as a paid practitioner or as one contributing services pro bono, is the legal malpractice insurance premium. These premiums vary in annual amount depending on the type of law practiced (lawyers who provide securities law opinions pay significantly higher premiums, for example), and the age and experience of the lawyer (premiums tend to rise as lawyers grow older). Premiums also increase each year to cover "prior acts." It must also be recognized that legal malpractice insurance policies are "claims-made policies," which means that a policy protects the insured only against those claims made in the year in which the policy is in force, regardless of when the alleged malpractice occurred. Consequently, a lawyer must keep a policy in force in each year following any year in which he or she last actually practiced, until the statute of limitations has run out for any potential claim. Since some clients may have a cause of action based on breach of contract, for which the statute in most jurisdictions is six years, the conservative lawyer would purchase malpractice coverage over that six-year period. That cost must be equated against the fees likely to be generated in the same time period.

Premium rates vary widely. In some states, at least one carrier would provide minimal coverage of $100,000 per claim, $300,000 aggregate, and $1,500 deductible, for a premium of $950 the first year, escalating at $350 per year, to $2,350 maximum in the fifth year. This carrier would provide coverage for part-time and pro bono work for a premium about 25 percent less in these jurisdictions.

Another carrier provided the author with premium quotations specific to Ohio and New York. These are applicable to single practitioners engaged in either real estate work or insurance defense. Real estate lawyers in Ohio and New York, with at least nine years of experience, would be charged an annual premium of $5,928 and $5,632, respectively, for $1 million (and $8,846 and $7,659 for $5 million) of coverage. Insurance defense lawyers in those states, with the same level of experience, would pay an annual premium of $2,863 and $3,990 for $1 million (and $8,846 and $7,649 for $5 million) of coverage. Real estate lawyers can buy malpractice coverage from this carrier for less in New York than in Ohio; however, litigators in Ohio pay lower premiums than litigators in New York.

Another underwriting group advised us that lower malpractice premiums are available in southern states and in smaller states, while the highest premiums are collected in states such as California. This group stated that, assuming "no prior acts" coverage, a policy with limits of $100,000 per claim and $300,000 in the aggregate, with a $1,000 deductible, would start at $350 per annum and go up to $2,000. It was stated that the premiums would increase each year to cover the "prior acts."

One large professional liability insurance company responded to the author's inquiry in some detail. This insurer provided a table, reproduced on page 23, and said that the annual premiums for various coverage options in the table are based on the following assumptions:

- Full prior acts coverage
- No paid claims within the past five years

- Practice limited to nonvolatile areas (no securities, syndications, or bank directorships, etc.)
- Being a solo practitioner
- An assumed state relativity of 1.00 ("average—relativities vary by state depending on the experience [of] all insured lawyers in the state")

This carrier said further that, since it does not offer a separate coverage form for part-time attorneys, the table assumes a full-time practice and the premiums are calculated accordingly.

PREMIUM TABLE
By Limit and Deductible

Limit		Deductible		
Per Claim	**Aggregate**	**$1,000**	**$2,500**	**$5,000**
$100,000	$300,000	$1,970	$1,891	$1,753
with FDD		2,049	1,970	1,931
$250,000	$250,000	$1,660	$2,581	$2,443
with FDD		2,738	2,660	2,620
$500,000	$500,000	$2,955	$2,876	$2,738
with FDD		3,034	2,955	2,916

Note: FDD = First dollar defense optional coverage

This carrier indicated that "in a reduced or part-time practice, our Underwriters will generally apply schedule credits to compensate for the reduced exposure posed to the Company." Such credits and debits are also applied to reflect the quality of the firm. One must recognize that the application of schedule credits or debits may result in higher or lower premiums than those reflected in the above table in which no credits are assumed.

While most lawyers are aware that practitioners in the field of securities law, and those dealing with substantial mergers and acquisitions, may be exposed to substantially higher premiums than others in the profession, it is not widely known that many other areas of the law call for higher malpractice insurance premiums. One carrier advised the author that among the "volatile areas," in addition to those mentioned above, are the following:

- Entertainment and sports
- Collection and repossession
- Corporate
- Estates and trusts
- Oil and gas
- Personal injury, plaintiff's side
- Real estate
- Taxation

Surcharges over basic premiums vary in amount depending upon the level of concentration of the attorney, if any, in the areas mentioned above. Premiums also differ, depending on whether the policy provides the first dollar of defense funds, as the table above indicates.

There is no quick and easy answer to the question, "How much must I pay for malpractice insurance?" Responsible carriers rate each attorney in a firm individually. The carriers that provided information to this author showed that premium costs could range from $350 annually in a small state in a low-risk practice, for $300,000 of coverage and a $1,000 deductible, all the way to $8,846 annually for a real estate lawyer in Ohio buying $5 million of protection.

Lawyers whose firms are insured for malpractice risks with many carriers are not permitted by those carriers to purchase individual "tail" policies to cover claims arising after these lawyers have left the firm; the "tail" policies are available only if all partners in the firm agree to purchase them. The CNA insurance group has now made individual "tail" policies available to any lawyer whose firm was insured under a CNA policy; the premium for an unlimited "tail" policy is about 230 percent of the premium attributed to the lawyer under the firm's policy.

Overhead Expenses

Other items of expense that a retired lawyer choosing to remain in practice can expect to have, many of which were absorbed by the corporation or law firm with which he or she was previously associated, include court maintenance-of-good-standing fees, bar association dues and, in the case of the single practitioner, subscription and usage fees for Lexis/Nexis, Westlaw, or other commercially available legal research services. These are costs peculiar to the legal community and are in addition to office operating costs in the general population, such as rent, secretarial salaries and benefits, office equipment purchase or rental, utilities, and telephone and fax services.

Few lawyers have sufficient retirement income to cover the expenses of ordinary living and still have enough left over to pay for these office operating costs. To continue to practice law in some form after retirement from a government position, a corporation, or a law firm usually means that the lawyer must be in a position to generate fees from his or her services. Not everyone is able to do so. This ability, or lack of it, is a factor deserving great weight when it comes to deciding on the course for a second career.

The economic hurdle is not impossible to overcome. The lawyer who chooses to provide legal services on a pro bono basis can find any number of organizations that can use his or her services, and these organizations will generally provide the umbrella of malpractice insurance coverage, but it is necessary to check to be sure such coverage is provided. It must be recognized, of course, that the coverage applies only to legal services rendered under the auspices of those organizations.

However, even the pro bono lawyer incurs costs that are not covered or reimbursed by the institution or organization. For example, the lawyer must continue to pay the attorney's occupational tax in the jurisdiction and may choose to remain a member of the state bar and to subscribe to a few legal services in order to remain current with developments in his or her area of practice. Some tax advantages may accrue to the lawyer in this arrangement. While the value of the lawyer's time may not be deducted for federal income tax purposes, expenses incurred in the donation of personal services—which would seem to include the items aforementioned—may be deducted.

Waivers of Occupational Taxes and Dues

In this connection, the lawyer who proposes to retire from active practice should learn the rules in his or her state with regard to the payment of the occupational tax and the applicable level of bar association dues. In a number of states, payment of the tax is waived and bar association dues are substantially reduced for lawyers who elect to retire and file the necessary statement with the designated state office or bar association.

Taxes on Retirement Plan Distributions

Taxes are an important element in calculating the amount of disposable income a retiree will have available, and this is especially true of the older senior lawyer. Many attorneys in the mid-1970s established a Keogh Plan to accumulate capital gain and income free of federal income tax: That tax is deferred until age seventy and a half. But, beginning in the year following the year in which that age is attained, a taxpayer must take down approximately 5 percent of the amount in the Keogh fund and pay tax on it at ordinary income rates.

What is important to remember here is that even though the Internal Revenue Service characterizes the amount removed from the combined IRA and Keogh accounts as "income" and taxes it at ordinary income rates, *it is not income at all*. It represents your capital. If you spend it, instead of reinvesting it (perhaps in tax-free bonds) to produce some income, it will be lost forever.

The effect on the item called "taxable income" and on the amount of tax payable is dramatic. Assume a married person has $200,000 in a Keogh account and reaches the critical year when he or she must begin to pay taxes. If that person has other taxable income of, say, $30,000, the tax at 1992 rates on that amount would be about $4,500. However, consider that there must be added 5 percent of $200,000, or $10,000, raising the tax bill by some $2,050. This person's "take home" amount (assuming the choice is to reinvest the amount removed from the IRA and Keogh) is reduced from about $25,500 to around $23,450.

Even persons with greater resources are not spared. Now assume a married person, who has accumulated $1 million in a Keogh account, and who reaches the tax-obligated age, has other taxable income of, say, $75,000. Absent the obligation to withdraw funds from the Keogh accounts, his or her federal income tax, ignoring possible deductions, would be about $16,346. However, the withdrawal obligation, which would apply to approximately 5 percent of the Keogh fund, or $50,000, would increase that person's federal income tax by $15,155. The anticipated $75,000 of spendable income (again, assuming that the amount withdrawn from the IRA and Keogh accounts will be reinvested) suddenly is reduced to $59,845.

When pondering the financial picture for retirement, this significant tax impact just from growing older must be recognized.

Additional Sources of Income

As the bottom line becomes clear, many who contemplate a second career may search for an opportunity that provides the prospective of additional income, albeit not at the same earnings level as in the first career. Among the possibilities: service as a full-time general counsel to a charitable organization; work as a mediator-arbitrator for one of the many entities that have been established in this field; serving as an expert witness; or teaching law as an adjunct professor. Each of these is discussed in some detail in this and later chapters.

Counseling Charitable Organizations

Many fairly substantial charitable organizations are neither quite big enough nor financially sound enough to employ legal counsel at what might be termed a competitive salary. However, if one is willing to work for something less than market rates, the possibilities of finding very interesting intellectual challenges abound. Locating such a position may require a bit of searching. Your local bar association may have a referral service; and charitable groups in your area, such as community trusts or the United Way, may know of member units that need legal counsel.

Arbitration and Mediation

Many retired lawyers elect to become arbitrators or mediators. While the American Arbitration Association does not expect that arbitrators from its National Panel will be compensated for a single day of service, a fee—negotiated by the AAA with the parties—is paid to an arbitrator for time in excess of one day. The fees paid by commercial organizations providing dispute resolution services are negotiated and vary depending upon the complexity of the matter, the experience of the arbitrator/mediator, and the time required to dispose of the dispute. (We discuss alternative dispute resolution at greater length in Chapter 9.)

Retired judges in many jurisdictions are permitted to sit in their own locales, and state law establishes their rates of compensation. In fact, some jurisdictions—Florida, for example—accord reciprocity to jurists from other states who desire to sit as trial referees.

In this sphere of work, there also is opportunity for the senior lawyer. Under the Civil Justice Reform Act of 1990, every federal district court is required to promulgate a plan to reduce the expense and delay in the administration of justice. The plan must consider and may include "authorization of alternative dispute resolution programs in appropriate cases" (28 USC § 473[a][6]). More than one-third of the districts have already adopted plans. This has resulted in establishment of pilot programs in a number of districts for Alternate Dispute Resolution systems under auspices of both state and federal courts. These programs utilize retired and senior judges and senior lawyers to sit as mediators. Where permitted by statute, the mediators will be paid "reasonable compensation." Opportunity for training will be provided in a number of districts to those lawyers who may wish to serve, and in some districts such training is mandatory.

The Bottom Line

No matter what you decide on as a second career, it is bound to cost money. For the younger person or the middle-aged person embarking on a new course, the choice, usually dictated by family need, favors an activity providing compensation. For the older lawyer, soon to retire or already retired, the choice is somewhat different: whether to engage in a pro bono activity or to do something that will provide income. Keep in mind what we said in Chapter 2: If you are retired, or about to retire, you should factor in a large measure of self-satisfaction, because to enjoy what you will be doing at little or no compensation may be more important than finding an activity that will provide income.

Regardless of your situation, it is important that you assess your resources carefully and analyze your anticipated expenditures in a potential second career; then reflect upon your needs and the needs of your family before you make your choice. Income from pensions, IRAs and Keoghs, and Social Security may appear adequate to cover your needs, so that supplemental earned income is unnecessary for you. Bear in mind, however, that every second career, even a pro bono position, involves expenses of some sort—perhaps additional costs for travel, automobile, parking, luncheons, periodical subscriptions, and the like. Factor those costs into the picture before you decide which second-career opportunity is economically feasible for you. There is no point in feeling the stress of finances when you are supposed to be "smelling the roses." If you cannot provide pro bono services comfortably, then seek a second career that will offer some remuneration to supplement your unearned income.

A Thought for the Younger Lawyer

Most of the discussion in this chapter centered on the lawyer who is retired, or about to retire, and his or her financial resources and their consequences regarding a second career. Those lawyers in a younger age bracket should take heed. It is time to think about saving—preparing for retirement, so that your second-career choices will not be constrained by your financial picture. You must recognize that some sacrifice at this stage in your life is necessary to make a better future.

For example, let us suppose you are age fifty-five. You have some savings that will generate investment income, and you will have Social Security; but you want to augment these sources by about $50,000 a year and you want to reach this goal by age seventy, when you expect to retire. Assuming that your savings now, and your nest egg when you retire, will have an 8 percent return overall, you will have to save slightly more than $1,800 a month (about $21,600 a year) to assemble the $625,000 in principal required to earn that $50,000. Satisfied with an additional $25,000 a year? Then you "only" have to save $900 a month!

These numbers are a bit frightening. But if you would like a second career requiring little or no financial underpinning, you need to think about accumulating a base—beginning today.

4

Psychological Matters

A career change is, indeed, an important event in your life. The decision whether or not to make a change—and what kind of career to choose—should be made, first, after reflection on your own concerns, abilities, and weaknesses; and second, consideration of its effect on others.

In the following section, Dr. Larry R. Richard discusses the first half of that equation.

Career Transitions after Age Fifty: Tips from a Career Counselor

Larry R. Richard

Larry Richard earned his Juris Doctor degree from the University of Pennsylvania Law School in 1972 and is a candidate for a Ph.D. in psychological studies from Temple University in 1994. He practiced law for ten years before founding Lawgistics in 1981. Since then, he has provided career counseling for hundreds of lawyers nationwide. Currently he is the president of Richard Consulting Group, Inc., a Philadelphia firm that provides management consulting services for law firms on issues in communication, motivation, and morale. His doctoral research investigated attorney job dissatisfaction and lawyers' personalities.

Career transitions are but a subset of the broader phenomenon of adult life transitions. Psychologists describe several stages of normal development through which the average adult passes. For most adults in their thirties and forties, the principal developmental task is what is known as "generativity," or the need to accomplish something of value, generally through one's career. Lawyers are no exception.

As you move beyond age fifty, it is typical to reassess your career and ask yourself the hard question of whether you have created what is, to you, meaningful. Any thoughts of a transition at this point in your career are often guided by the desire for completion, the desire to fulfill those areas of your life as yet unfulfilled. These may include further professional accomplishment, time for hobbies or family, volunteer work, a new career entirely, or simply more of the same.

If you are a typical senior lawyer who is considering a career change, you should be aware that during this phase of your life it is perfectly natural to begin wondering how you can meet your own personal needs for fulfillment through your daily work life. For many individuals, this leads to a shift from a career whose main purpose was income production to one whose main purpose is individual fulfillment. This may take the form of turning an avocation into a vocation, or of cutting back one's work load to get more involved in community service. Others see it as a time to give back through teaching some of what they learned during their years of practice.

Shifting one's perspective in this way is not without its complications. Many lawyers, upon reaching this stage in their lives, find it somewhat daunting to give up the comfort of the structure that the full-time practice of law has provided. Added to this for many is an unfamiliar uncertainty, a lack of clarity, about career goals.

In my own experience in working with senior attorneys, I find that an exploration of one's vocational values can be an excellent tool for providing the internal compass that one needs at this time to know which direction is the right one. If you are a typical senior lawyer who is considering a career change, you may find it helpful to have a model to guide your decision making.

Career Anchors

One model that I have used for many years is the Career Anchors model developed by Professor Edgar Schein at the Sloan School of Management at M.I.T. Dr. Schein identified eight core values that seem to serve as the "glue" that holds someone in a job. For any one individual, usually only one of these values is the "bottom line" value. There may be one, two, or even three of the other values that also seem important, but for most people only one is held so deeply and strongly that it can be said to arise from your identity.

Here are Schein's eight core values, or "Career Anchors," adapted for lawyers, plus two others that I have encountered in working with lawyers over the years:

Security Anchor. If this is your "anchor," then the main thing that a job can provide for you, and the main way that it can "feed" your identity, is to offer tenure, continuity, predictability, and security. For most people embracing this category, the kind of security they seek is financial, but others get a very similar need met by finding geographical security (establishing roots in the community), emotional security (getting to know a familiar cast of characters), or intellectual security (developing an expertise in a subject that makes you marketable).

Lawyers with a security anchor may have already gravitated toward jobs like government lawyer, partner in a well-established firm that views growth and expansion conservatively, tenured law faculty position, or the like. If you identify with the security anchor more than any other anchor, and you are not currently in a job that meets this value, a sensible career move at this time would be to find a position that offers some kind of tenure.

Autonomy Anchor. If the most important criterion for a job is the degree of personal freedom you are accorded, then your bottom-line value may be the autonomy anchor. Lawyers with this value like to call the shots in handling their own cases and do not like to be told what to do or how to do it. If you identify with the autonomy anchor more than any other anchor, and you are not currently in a job that meets this value, a sensible career move at this time would be to find a position that above all gives you the occupational independence you've been missing. For some this may mean going solo, for others it may mean becoming the director of a nonprofit organization, and for some others it may simply mean becoming of counsel to your firm.

Entrepreneurial Anchor. Individuals with this particular anchor place a great deal of value on creativity and building something from scratch. "Entrepreneurial" in this sense is used in the very broadest sense of the word to mean not just "starting up a new venture" but in general the process of developing something from scratch. Examples include the lawyer who prides himself or herself on creative drafting of pleadings, leases, appellate briefs, etc.; the plaintiff's personal injury lawyer who continually finds clever ways to cobble together various coverages to yield a large recovery; the lawyer involved in setting up innovative CLE programs; and so on.

If you identify with the entrepreneurial anchor more than any other anchor, and you are not currently in a job that meets this value, a sensible career move at this time might be to start a new venture that your expertise equips you for, or get involved with the development of an innovative program in bar activities, legal education, charitable work, or the business community; or develop a subsidiary enterprise that fits with your legal specialty. (Lawyers have established real estate development firms, public relations firms, investment banking firms, investment groups, employment advisory groups, government compliance consulting firms, environmental consulting firms, and the like, as subsidiary ventures to their law practice.)

General Manager Anchor. Ed Schein once called this the "Harvard MBA" anchor. It describes the individual who identifies with being a tough decision maker, and who enjoys the tasks that Peter Drucker described as key for a manager—planning, organizing, staffing, directing, controlling, and problem solving. If this is your anchor, you probably enjoy power, achievement, and success. It has been my experience that lawyers with this career anchor would much rather be involved in the business world, like many of their clients, than in the day-to-day practice of law. If you identify with the general manager anchor more than any other anchor, and you are not currently in a job that meets this value, a sensible career move at this time might be to consider a move in-house so you can get closer to a business environment, especially in a company with a track record of lawyers gravitating into the ranks of management. Alternatively, if you have strong business law experience, you may be able to capitalize on this credential and move directly into a business position, although in recent years it has become tougher for lawyers to make this kind of move without one or two intermediate steps.

Craft Anchor. If you personally identify with an actual craft, skill, or calling, this is your anchor. If you *wish* you had a craft that you called your very own, chances are good that one of the other anchors will fit you better. Why? People with a true craft anchor generally know what their work identity is already. Unfortunately for the rest of us, society perpetuates a myth that job satisfaction will follow if you can just gaze into the crystal ball and figure out what it is that you were really meant to do. For most of us, the "what" does not take the form of a particular calling, as it does for the person with a craft anchor, but rather ends up being a "how" (e.g., security, autonomy, etc.).

If your anchor is craft, and the craft is practicing law, you are likely to be sorely disappointed if you retire or change careers at this point in your life. You are better advised to cut back on your hours or switch to a less demanding environment but remain in practice. On the other hand, if you identify with the craft anchor more than any other anchor, you are currently practicing, and your craft is something other than the practice of law (teacher, writer, historian, political scientist, etc.), a sensible career move at this time might be to consider a true career change—into your identified craft—if you can afford the drop in income. If you can't, you are strongly urged to cut back on your hours to the extent realistically possible so as to create some leisure time during which you can develop your craft as an avocation, if you haven't already done so.

Principle Anchor. If you are driven by a cause, a principle, a dogma, or an idea, then this is your bottom-line value. Those with a principle anchor go to work in order to actively further what they believe in. Principles can be broadly or narrowly drawn. You might identify broadly with protecting the underdog, or more narrowly with advocating specifically on behalf of the rights of one-armed blind parakeets. Whatever the principle, most people with this anchor would agree that practicing law yields its principal satisfaction not from the inherent nature of law practice (that would be a craft), but rather because it is a good vehicle (one of many) for promoting the principle in which you believe. Examples of this value in action include the lawyer who fervently believes in being an activist to protect the environment and lives that principle by working as an environmental litigator, or the historic preservationist who practices municipal law as a way of actualizing his or her viewpoint.

If you identify with the principle anchor more than any other anchor, and you are not currently in a job that meets this value, a sensible career move at this time might be to consider a move that allows you to spend the main part of your day in furtherance of your valued principle. A number of my post-fifty clients have begun positioning themselves to become directors of various charitable organizations promoting causes such as preventing child abuse, helping the homeless, preserving forestation, improving waste treatment plants, and providing meals to the elderly. Since there are a very limited number of these positions, the transition strategy is usually a stepwise one, rather than a single leap from law practice to directorship.

Pure Challenge Anchor. Do you love the rush of adrenaline that comes from adventure, risk, or danger? If you prize this feeling more than any of the other values described here, then the pure challenge anchor may be your bottom-line value. People with this anchor often choose a work life of physicality—professional football or basketball players, the pro tennis or golf tour, putting out oil fires in the North Sea, being a stunt person in Hollywood, etc. But pure challenge can be earned with brains as well as with brawn: real estate developers, investment bankers, dealmakers in general, plaintiff's personal injury attorneys handling high-risk cases—these all qualify. While this is not one of the more common career anchors for lawyers, it is shared by a number of your colleagues. If you identify with the pure challenge anchor more than any other anchor, and you are not currently in a job that meets this value, the idea of making a "sensible" career move at this point might seem a bit boring to you. You may wish to consider how you can add more adventure to your life, either by adopting a marketing strategy that positions you as a specialist in the most difficult and challenging cases in your area of expertise, or by moving into one of the riskier occupational niches referred to above. This kind of transition is not for the faint-hearted.

Life-Style Anchor. If you've been reading along so far and wondering, "But what about me?," the life-style anchor may be for you. While the first seven anchors are all about your work life in some respect, the life-style anchor is held by those whose main interest is a balanced life-style. For people with the life-style anchor, one's work is only a part—sometimes only a small part—of the overall living experience. More important is leisure time, time with family, a relaxing pace, volunteer work, hobbies, spirituality, or balance of all the pieces. If life-style is your anchor, you probably go to work more out of a sense of duty than joy. It's your life after work that matters more, and ideally your job serves your life in some way, and not vice versa. If you identify with the life-style anchor more than with any other anchor, and you are not currently in a job that meets this value, a sensible career move at this time might be to consider retirement or dramatically reducing your hours. Some lawyers with this anchor seek to work for organizations where they can work a nine-to-five day and have ample vacation time. Still others go out on their own.

Other Anchors

I have found that some lawyers don't really identify too strongly with any of the eight career anchors listed above. The following two anchors were not part of Professor Schein's original research but rather have emerged from my own work with hundreds of lawyers over the years:

Effectiveness Anchor. If the real reason you do what you do is that you love to feel that you are having an impact, that your work truly affects the lives of people, that you are effective, and you feel more passionately about this than about the eight values just described, then this is your anchor. If you identify with the effectiveness anchor more than any other anchor, and you are not currently in a job that meets this value, a sensible career move at this time might be to consider working for a firm with greater clout, running for political office, working behind the scenes for your favorite politician, or campaigning to become the head of a bar or other professional association.

Intellectual Challenge Anchor. This anchor is distinguished from the "pure challenge" anchor described above in the following way: A person interested in "pure challenge" likes the rush of adrenaline which might be available, for example, in putting together a complex corporate transaction (as a dealmaker not as a draftsman). A person interested in "intellectual challenge," on the other hand, is more of a jurist at heart. It's not the adrenaline surge that matters so much as the stimulation of the higher cerebral function of the brain. If you loved the jurisprudence of law school much more than the humdrum routine of actual practice, then this may be your anchor. If you identify with the intellectual challenge anchor more than any other anchor, and you are not currently in a job that meets this value, a sensible career move at this time might include the following options: Consider seeking a position as a law professor; volunteer to teach some CLE programs; write a legal treatise in your specialty; become active in committee work for the American Bar Association or any professional trade association or juridical society that embraces your area of interest; seek a position with a think tank; consider college teaching; or explore ways to move from law into public administration.

Concluding Thoughts

If you are contemplating a change in your job or your career, bear in mind that the guidelines offered in this chapter focused on just one of several factors that you should consider before making a move. (For a more detailed discussion of the other factors, read my chapter entitled "Matching the Job with Your Personality" in the 1993 ABA book *Breaking Traditions*.)

I also recommend that you consult a qualified career counselor in your local area, especially one who has experience in assisting lawyers in general and senior lawyers in particular.

The whole idea behind using a model like the career anchors concept is to match your job to your own needs so you experience a high degree of congruence. Many lawyers sacrifice this congruence earlier in their careers in order to satisfy more practical needs. As you move into the status of "senior lawyer," you may find your needs changing. You may feel that it's time that you met your more personal needs for self-development and expression, growth and relaxation. By prioritizing your values and identifying which of the ten career anchors most centrally fits your own identity, hopefully you will have a better sense of what kind of change you need to seek at this point in your life. Good luck!

Having read Dr. Richard's description of the analysis you must make of yourself in order to decide the issue of a career change, let us assume that you have come to the conclusion that a change is in order. Any person contemplating such a change readily concedes that there are personal difficulties to be faced and dealt with. In a conversation with Judge Glenn Robert Lawrence, Dr. Isaiah Zimmerman, a psychologist who has counseled judges and practicing lawyers, examines some of the psychological problems a career change may present: leaving a position of influence and authority, the effect of reductions in prestige and power, the viewpoint of associates.

Dr. Zimmerman points out the necessity of presenting a proper image of oneself to others when making a career change, and he discusses the importance of stating the reason clearly and truthfully when talking with one's friends and associates. (Note: The following transcript was edited by the author of this book.)

Psychological Issues in Career Change

Isaiah Morris Zimmerman

Dr. Isaiah Morris Zimmerman is a clinical psychologist with a practice in Washington, D.C. He received his bachelor's (1951) and master's (1953) degrees from the University of California at Berkeley and a Ph.D. degree from the Catholic University of America (1967). From 1953 until 1966, he served as a psychologist with the United States Air Force, which awarded him the Air Force Commendation Medal for his work.

In 1966, Dr. Zimmerman entered private practice. He now serves as a consultant to, or is on the board of directors of, various state, federal, and private institutions, including the Arlington (Va.) Mental Health Center, the District Court of Massachusetts, the Administrative Office of the Courts and the Judicial Council of Utah, the Group Psychotherapy Foundation, and the International Association of Group Psychotherapy.

Dr. Zimmerman is on the faculty of the National Judicial College, the Washington School of Psychiatry, and the Medical School of George Washington University. He lectures frequently to lawyers and judges of both trial and appellate courts concerning judicial stress management, appellate collegial relations, and judicial productivity. Dr. Zimmerman says, "I am very concerned about the stress under which so many lawyers and judges work."

JUDGE LAWRENCE: Good morning, Dr. Zimmerman! We are here in your lovely home and office. We are discussing this morning what a lawyer is to do when he or she decides that maybe, just maybe, it's time for a career change. We are particularly interested in your viewpoint as a psychologist: What kind of psychological issues would a man or woman face? How should these psychological issues be managed so one does not become deeply mired in problems?

DR. ZIMMERMAN: The first thing that is important to realize is that when a person contemplates retirement, it sometimes carries the specter of approaching old age and one's ultimate demise. These are the thoughts that people want to ignore, because the contemplation of one's ending brings with it a profound desire to reassess: "What have I spent my years doing? Has it been worthwhile? Did I have much effect? Did I help people or society?" In particular, since I have done so much work with the judiciary, I have observed that judges tend to be extremely conscientious, somewhat idealistic people. Despite their often hard exterior, they are beset with questions: "What have I produced or left behind in this world? Has it been effective? Will anybody remember my name?" And there are also questions of the assessment of one's personal life: "How has my time been spent with my family, with my close friends, with my children?" So a profound reassessment is part of setting the stage for a new course in life.

In our culture, since we tend to be technology-oriented and professions like the law are inundated with all sorts of administrative detail and responsibility, people tend to escape into reviewing their plans for their future, reviewing their investments, where they should live in retirement, what future real estate values will be in some particular part of Florida or Arizona. All these questions, of course, are practical and very important, but they tend to form a curtain, obscuring the more profound issues that have to be faced. Whenever I have been an advisor to judges and lawyers contemplating retirement, I have certainly encouraged them to do practical planning. But gradually I have gently steered them back to take the time to face these important, deeper questions about life and how it has been conducted up to this point, and when, where, why, and how—but mostly why—should it be changed.

And, of course, all people have a personal script, perhaps it should be called a fantasy, about their later years. Some people—I am just going to point out a few scripts that I have come across; it doesn't exhaust the universe of scripts by any means—some people have a driving ambition to retire early almost as a competitive edge. "I retired at forty-five which meant I had to have a lot of money by forty-five or fifty in order not to have to work anymore." That becomes an absolute goal. Others have no interest in retiring; they want to continue their work, take senior status or something, but they want to keep a hand in; they love to work, and they have no desire to retire fully.

Another script is to move to a physically more appealing area and have less stress from weather, etc., and to continue virtually full-time in that area so that you do the same thing but you do it in much more pleasant circumstances. You move from windy, blustery Chicago to Laguna Beach in California and carry on a small law practice there.

So, the scripts are very important.

As far as timing is concerned, I have advised—and find it very important—that a person, man or woman, begin addressing these issues about two or three years ahead. It takes as many as two or three years to determine one's wishes, see how realistic they are, and begin to make the necessary practical arrangements.

I don't mean to deride practical arrangements, but I do believe they have to be integrated within the larger picture and the overview of one's life. In the course of these two or three years of contemplating retirement or change of profession or vocation, a person must discuss it with close friends, with the spouse, and other family members, since his or her change affects these people. It affects them not only practically, in terms of money, opportunity to visit, and so forth, but it also affects their image of themselves, because one's self-worth is tied up very much with the images of the people who are significant to us.

Certainly, being able to visit, being able to drop in, being able to spend holidays with each other, is very important. If a person moves far away, he or she can drop out of others' lives; so these others desire to have some say in the decision, or at least be emotionally prepared for it.

Also, in such moves there is a profound and wrenching change that has to do with one's social, professional, and personal support network. As they contemplate change, judges, lawyers, and others are really contemplating leaving their comfortable set of friends, relatives, and people they rely on for various kinds of support. They perhaps move to an area where maybe nobody knows them and they have to begin from scratch, and that is a big stressor, because beginning a whole new social network is very stressful.

That's why so many people, as they get older and think of changing work, changing residence, and going into semiretirement, tend to drift to where some of their old friends already are living. They form a little colony. These little colonies exist all over the country, and overseas, too. There are clusters of American expatriates who have joined their friends in a little artistic village in Mexico, in Costa Rica, in the south of France, or wherever. Usually, these are accretions of previous friends and acquaintances, so there is some knowledge of what to expect and what kind of life and what kind of economic circumstance prevails in these places.

With all this comes the interior journey, the interior change that I mentioned earlier—and that also takes two or three years to face. Some go into counseling or therapy for a while, not because they have "a problem" but because they want a thoroughly expert and neutral person with whom to explore some of their ideas and feelings. They need to be able to talk without any inhibition about some of their regrets and some of their feelings and not disturb those who are close to them. At any rate, the deeper inside journey has to do with the contemplation of eventual death and eventual physical aging and the end of one's life.

So, it is important for the retiree to have support and to have access to a brave soul who, as a companion in time, can face these issues and discuss them frankly.

For example, in terms of script, a man may be feeling his age and feeling that he is getting somewhat infirm and yet he is tied to his status, his income source, his place in society; he doesn't want to lose his significance because social significance is usually quite important to us all. To move to a new place where nobody knows you, your income is limited, and you are not relevant or important to anybody else is a big shock. People need to review and reinforce themselves. They must ask how can they let go of their status and their image or their role and adopt a new one. Again, that isn't easy or something that we base purely on practicalities, such as saying, "Well, I've always loved boats. If I invest in a little boatyard, I can make so many thousands a year and live in a nice place and that takes care of it."

No, that is not enough. You have to understand the deeper significance of that decision to yourself and to those who, perhaps, will move with you. Also, in this deeper journey, we have to look at the significance that looking back places on one's prior work. For example, if a person makes a profound change, what does it say about his previous years? Let's say that a person leaves the law and becomes an artist, then starts to sell paintings. Should he or she have been an artist all along? Should this person have stayed with art, if that was his or her youthful vocation before the law? There are these retrospective questions that arise, and they are worth discussing. They are not silly speculation. They are worth considering, because one must reassess one's life. "What did I do? Why did I do it? Where am I now?" And one must assess the significance of that particular sequence. Human beings are sequencing creatures, and they need to make sense of their sequence. If people feel out of phase, out of sequence, or if a couple feels out of phase, out of sequence, that can be very difficult and stressful.

For example, there are many, many divorced people in our society. Very often, the second marriage poses an out-of-sequence pairing of lives, for example, an older man and a somewhat younger woman. She may be hitting her stride in her business or vocation, and he wants to start retiring. That is a definite stressor to them, and they need to take time to discuss, assess, compromise, and try to work something out.

Also, with more and more women entering the professions and business, it is no longer assumed that a woman will move when a man moves, even in his retirement or change of vocation. Older men find that they are moving to follow the careers of their younger wives, and they have to make an adjustment and find something significant themselves in her new job location.

All these factors have to be taken into account as a person contemplates a change.

I think, numerically—I don't have statistical hard data, but numerically—most people, because of today's economic circumstances and the way our culture is developing, think more of change, more of reduction of work, rather than retirement as such. I don't think that many people totally retire, play golf, go fishing, get up late in the morning, read the paper, or go look at the stock quotations—that is a minority. I think the majority of both men and women really have a desire to be doing something significant through all their years. But in light of the discomfort of approaching old age, they would like to do it in a more comfortable setting and to work fewer hours and have less of a demand, but nonetheless do significant work. I, myself, as a therapist, have had the privilege of talking and working with a number of men and women who have retired in their late fifties or early sixties and found it profoundly uncomfortable to just "do nothing" or just enjoy the fruits of their prior investments. They have returned as consultants, as advisors, to small business associations, and have also returned to the active pursuit of business or law or some other vocation full-time. They love it, really love it, and they have a second wind, so to speak. They need a fresh start, and so all these new things are fascinating. People have all sorts of different scripts and solutions. These are my thoughts.

Would you like to ask me some questions?

JUDGE LAWRENCE: Thank you so much, Dr. Zimmerman. You've given us almost a mini-encyclopedia on how to approach this career change question. A couple of things occurred to me. First, I think many men and women, when they look to changing a career, say, "Well, I am trying to escape from a painfully competitive atmosphere." Consider, for instance, a lawyer in a large firm who is a "rainmaker," and he has to produce umpteen billable hours every month in order to meet the expenses of the firm. That is a pretty high-pressure activity. How do you see this personality, who has been very successfully competitive for a large span of his life, now switching gears?

DR. ZIMMERMAN: The first thing is honesty with oneself. Most of us have a tendency to stay in whatever is comfortable and keep the role, the status, and the niche we occupy. So it is very important to be able to slow down, to look inside oneself, and to reflect on the need for change. We may be getting internal signals for many, many years that it is important to slow down, change, make a shift; still, we may ignore these signals and proceed as though everything is going fine with no internal contradictions.

The other aspect here is the significance of one's work to oneself; perhaps, as you mentioned, a person may be a "rainmaker." A rainmaker usually has enormous pride in his or her ability to produce income to attract clients. The idea of going into teaching or going into some other line of work where this particular quality will not necessarily be prized involves giving up a certain picture of oneself and the pride one has in this kind of achievement and skill. That is something that people often resist and deny, and brush under the rug.

The other factor that comes to mind is that the so-called rainmaker is only a rainmaker in his particular milieu; put him somewhere else, and he is no longer a rainmaker. He has to find an alternative significance, so he may seek it in some status-laden job or in doing something very altruistic, such as becoming a fundraiser for a children's hospital or for some other cause. Then, the rainmaker can continue to use those skills, but for a totally different purpose and in a totally different structure. There are many ways of continuing to use one's specific skills in another context.

JUDGE LAWRENCE: When we approach a change, and you have been alluding to this—perhaps you can spell it out in somewhat greater detail—there seems to be a bit of fantasy. How does fantasy play a part in reorienting ourselves to another career?

DR. ZIMMERMAN: Fantasy is a remarkable gift and capacity that people have. It's the first step in any kind of creative decision making. People who are restricted in their fantasies, or who judge their fantasies, or don't allow them to go forth somewhat, are severely handicapped. It is very important to have freedom to exchange fantasies. That is what I alluded to earlier when I mentioned the word "script." The fantasy writes the script, and it is useful among friends, among people you trust, who are not going to be judgmental or who are not going to be in some oppression, to listen to you without any prejudgment, without any interruption, and have you spin out your fantasy.

Fantasies are very important, also, to put into some kind of form. Sometimes one can speak one's fantasies into a tape recorder, or one can write notes or keep a little diary. One might say:

> My fantasies, my daydreams have been changing. I used to think of leaving my franchise business and going into high-school teaching, or I was thinking of leaving teaching and going into some other kind of proprietorship type of business, but I find that the more I go into this fantasy, the clearer it becomes. It is like something emerging through murky water, and what really interests me is the excitement of that particular dream. It has to do with, say, being a partner. I have been solo all my life. I am really looking for a partner. Maybe I could have a partnership with my wife or with an old friend, but I am finding that the core of the fantasy is that I am tired of working alone. I want to work with someone else.

So that is part of the illuminating function that a fantasy can have. Fantasies are fundamental to plans to change one's vocation.

JUDGE LAWRENCE: When we get older, there are unquestionably physiological changes, and I am wondering to some extent if the psychological fires start to bank or if we are either stuck or gifted with the same drives and complexes and predilections that we have had from our youth up to our middle years. Is there a timetable that we should be watching in some manner?

DR. ZIMMERMAN: First of all, I would like to emphasize that, as we know, but, as we often forget, people are unique and are full of surprises. I have worked with people professionally for forty years now, and I never, never cease to be amazed at the incredible resourcefulness, creativity, and variety of the human experience.

Second, indeed as we grow older, our basic personality doesn't change, but our view of the world changes. One of the most profound changes is that one becomes less and less what I would call omnipotent. Younger people tend to be somewhat omnipotent; they believe that nothing bad can happen to them. They can achieve almost anything. That is a very necessary and exciting world view, even though it can certainly get you into trouble unless it is balanced out by prudence and education. But as one grows older—I would say probably somewhere in the middle forties, early fifties—one has a world view that includes an appreciation of one's limitations, of the limitation of the environment, and the economic and social situation. Therefore, planning is a little bit prudent and less prone to what I call omnipotent thoughts and feelings.

Also, as one grows older, in the late forties, early fifties, one begins to think of the approaching end of one's life and begins to reassess, begins to look at the "worthwhileness" of how one is spending one's time. Even though you have been very successful in a particular line of work, you may always have had an edge of dissatisfaction and frustration with it, and a dream long held back starts to creep up closer to the surface.

For example, I know one psychiatrist who loves to cook and often had the dream of owning a restaurant. Well, his dream surfaced with such strength that he retired in his early fifties and went into the restaurant business, and now he is very happy. He came into his own, or came out of the closet, as a chef and a restaurant owner and has no desire to reduce his work hours.

Another aspect of aging is the joint dream and wish of a couple. I think it is very important, since the majority of people are coupled, that the fantasies, dreams, and joint wishes of the couple be explored. When one thinks of a middle-aged couple, indeed, there is a great need to be aware of early fantasies, because they often come back later in life with great force, and we find that they have been lying there undisturbed, strong though latent, for the past twenty, thirty years.

JUDGE LAWRENCE: A new career is beckoning to you and you have to make a decision whether to say yes or no. How do you make a psychological assessment—and you have alluded to consulting your associates, your spouse, and your children—but how do you make sure the ultimate decision is psychologically right for you? With this question, I am keeping in mind the fact that many people warn against the pressures of change, and they point to the specter of the man who has made radical changes and quickly dies or rapidly deteriorates. How does one do the accounting, so to speak, psychologically, and know whether to say yes or no?

DR. ZIMMERMAN: That is a very interesting question. I think that, in addition to consulting with the people who care about you and know you quite well, it is very important to assess the foundations of your self-esteem, because ultimately our resourcefulness in the face of stress and in the face of a possible mistake relates to our self-esteem, which is a most important factor in our favor. And so, one has to bolster and refresh one's self-esteem.

For example, one must begin to look at one's fundamental worth, which is not linked to a particular job or status, and realize that one has intrinsic worth and value apart from job and status and from work history; that is very fundamental. In that realization, people may turn for spiritual and religious guidance. People will go to church or synagogue and ask God for some help or some wisdom. That is very important to fundamental self-worth.

Also, in order to make this big decision, there has to be an incipient forgiveness, that if I make a mistake, I will forgive myself. I will pick up the pieces and either move back to where I came from or do something else, but I will take this risk with eyes open, and also be prepared to forgive myself if it turns out to be a mistake—or even a disaster. Particularly between husband and wife, it is important to say, "Can we forgive ourselves; can we pick up the pieces, realize that we are not omnipotent and omniscient, and we may have to lick our wounds and regroup?" That is very important, this attitude of prior forgiveness.

Another aspect of self-esteem is a feeling of adventure that maybe one has been very cautious all of one's life, but now is the time one can venture out. Maybe there is a little bit of capital available for financial support, and there is confidence based on experience and the adventure appears to be worth it, and so you take that plunge. When you are actually close to making a decision, I would say that the combination of review, self-esteem, a prior commitment to forgiveness in case one has made a mistake, and the support of people who are close to you all play a very significant role. I think that is more fundamental than having a long checklist of pluses and minuses and weighing all these things. That may be necessary and useful to do, but the other factors, I think, are much more fundamental.

JUDGE LAWRENCE: That's very helpful, Dr. Zimmerman. Assume with me that a person has made the change. What is society going to be saying to the person who was a senior partner of a large firm and is now taking on a small practice in a country setting, or was a general counsel of a large corporation and is now going to work as of counsel to a law firm that offers very limited compensation and limited perquisites? What is society going to be saying, and what are we going to be saying to ourselves about such a change?

DR. ZIMMERMAN: That is a very important point. The first thing is that the private meaning inside oneself is not necessarily going to line up with the external message sent to outsiders, whether they are in the office and the community or in one's extended family. Only over time will one probably line up the private vision and the external image. So one has to be charitable and realistic and say, "If I move from a high corporate position to a small law firm in a New England town or be of counsel to some law firm, the image I project and my own dreams and my own reasons for making the move will not line up."

You have to be realistic and not expect them to line up for some time, until people get to know you and you establish yourself in a new social and professional network. The most usual experience is a feeling of threat, of anxiety, and that is where the stressor comes from inside—from fear of loss of status, of significance, and of importance. Sometimes feelings and the message can take a derogatory turn. "Oh, maybe they got rid of him. He wasn't really cutting the mustard anymore, or maybe he is a secret alcoholic, or maybe he committed some transgression and this is his way of sort of hiding out and spending his last years in peace or something." So there can be a derogatory image sometimes, developed completely innocently, without any justification.

In our culture, people generally tend to be rather competitive and achievement-oriented. For example, the younger members of the new setting—the office, workplace, corporation, or whatever—will feel a need to come to terms with this older person who is making this big change. They will have to size the person up and test him or her out and see why did he or she make this move. What is the real story? Do we respect that person's accumulated experience and presumed wisdom or is he or she on the way down and has very little to offer? They may think that all he or she has to offer are some connections but nothing much of substance. So the conclusion is that the person is being retained only for those connections.

All of this has to be worked through, and it takes at least a year or two to work through the adjustment between one's intended change and the net effect of this change on the people with whom the person is now working and living. So that is a very, very complex process.

JUDGE LAWRENCE: Carry it one step further. Of course, if your change worked out and your self-esteem remained intact, or you found a new vehicle for self-esteem, then, I would take it, Doctor, that in that case you are saying there is no great concern about that situation. But let's take the other side of the coin. Assume the competition is overpowering or the financing of your change has not worked out. Not enough business is coming in to make the thing workable. What kind of moves should a person make when the possibilities have been fully explored and they no longer engender any hope?

DR. ZIMMERMAN: As I said prior to this, you must build in an aspect of forgiveness and a flexibility that this is a calculated move. It's a calculated risk, and if things are not working out financially, recognizing that one's span of years ahead is shortening, one must make a rapid decision to get out of a situation that isn't working and try something else. So again, I have witnessed, in my course of work as a psychologist and psychotherapist, people in midlife making two or three rather significant moves in the space of a few years. Some may look askance at them and say, "Why is that person making all these changes?" Well, usually for economic reasons. It may turn out that there is not enough income and they have to adjust quickly. They can't just stay there and assume business gradually will pick up. So the decision making has to be rapid and the change may be quite drastic, and that is a very big stress on the person who is making the change and on his or her family. Another factor in all this is that the professional and social support one hoped for may not be there, so that, in addition to the economic factor, there is often a factor of incompatibility. At first impression, one might have thought that this was a nice, peaceful practice in a medium-sized town and that one could play golf after 4:00 in the afternoon—and it turns out to be quite different. There is a lot of competitiveness in this world, and there are political aspects to all this. The dream one had and the impression one had after careful investigation may have been quite erroneous, and one may seem to have entered a nest of vipers or something. So one again has to engage in some more rapid decision making and move on.

JUDGE LAWRENCE: Does a person, in the course of changes such as we have been discussing, need to cultivate some sort of image for the outside world?

DR. ZIMMERMAN: It is very important, particularly for professional and business people, to think through a kind of public relations spin or public relations image to convert a curriculum vitae from the way one promotes oneself with prospective employers or partners to the way one introduces oneself socially and businesswise in the new setting and to state the reason one gives for leaving the prior setting.

It is very important to be smart in a public relations sense and to present a fairly consistent picture that is not going to be shot full of holes by other facts that contradict it. For example, let's say a so-called rainmaker in a large law firm wants to move to a less-strenuous, less-demanding position in a middle-sized town and also wants to have a little bit more leisure time to play with the grandchilden who may live near this town. It's important to present a consistent public relations picture, not a falsification, but a picture that allows the bridging between the old and the new to proceed with dignity and meaningfulness. So this ex-rainmaker may, for example, formulate a basic picture that he conveys that he has been very, very pleased with his career up to this point, but is now ready for something new. "I want to be near my grandchildren, so we moved to this area." He shouldn't say, "I want to move to a smaller town where things will be less demanding." That may, it seems to me, not reflect well on him.

But if a person wants to move to where his or her grandchildren are and to take a hand in a different kind of law practice, this may present a much more coherent picture than something else. So it is useful to have a consistent public image.

JUDGE LAWRENCE: In making a change, is there an ideally mature perspective, from a psychological point of view?

DR. ZIMMERMAN: Yes, that is an interesting point. In my view, or my theoretical outlook, it is crucial to have meaning and self-esteem based on one's philosophical position in this world and the way one addresses the world. On top of that are the, I would say, more superficial—important, but more superficial—things like the kind of uniform we wear. I relate closely to the notion of career change because I spent ten years in the Air Force before shifting to my private practice. It was very important for me, and I had the benefit of some good therapy, so that I fundamentally see myself as Isaiah Zimmerman. What I have to offer the world is Isaiah Zimmerman. Whether I offer it in the blue uniform of the Air Force or whether I offer it in the business suit of a psychologist is secondary, so I think it is fundamental to have a core identity that one is proud of and from which one addresses the world, the generations, the people, the intimate lives that one is involved in, and then one thinks of a change of vocation as a very necessary but secondary layer of one's identity. Then, as one changes identity of work, the fundamental layers are still there—who one is. Although you chose to move to another phase, move to something different that intrigues you, you don't abandon your fundamental self.

JUDGE LAWRENCE: Dr. Zimmerman, thank you very much.

DR. ZIMMERMAN: It was a pleasure talking with you, and I wish you all the best.

Having been given a lesson in self-analysis by Dr. Richard and advised as to the consequences of a career change decision by Dr. Zimmerman, you need now to consider the various avenues open to you. By applying the advice of these eminent counselors, you should be better able to reach the proper conclusion.

5

Remaining in Law Practice

Many lawyers seeking a second career find a simple resolution to their problems: remain in law practice, but change the circumstances. For those in a large firm, it may mean moving to a smaller office; and for the single practitioners and attorneys practicing in small firms, relief may come from joining a larger organization. Some lawyers, unhappy with restrictions of any firm, small or large, may opt to hang out a shingle.

Moving from a Large Firm to a Small Firm

Younger lawyers, dissatisfied with the pressure of long hours and heavy work loads typical of large firm practice, may decide to shift to a smaller office. What problems does this career change create?

First, the smaller office may not necessarily work fewer hours or place lighter burdens upon its attorneys. Consequently, an attorney should not *assume* that this will be the case. An in-depth investigation of the nature of the work of the smaller firm and of the characteristics of its clients is imperative. A small boutique firm representing, say, professional athletes may find that its clients are calling for advice from far points of the globe at all hours. Another firm, whose specialty is defense of product liability claims, may find that its clients are sued often and unpredictably and need legal advice in coping with media inquiries on very short notice to its lawyers. On the other hand, a smaller firm practicing in the tax area may find that it is extremely busy for a relatively brief period but that its attorneys can live a fairly normal existence in the remainder of the year.

The lawyer shifting from a large firm to a small one must also consider the desires of his or her own clients. Many corporations, particularly those without sizable legal staff, prefer to do business with a large firm that can provide service in a wide variety of disciplines. On the other hand, clients will prefer to deal with a small firm in these situations: (1) in a significant matter where the small firm has particular expertise and substantial staff support is not required to deal with the problem, and (2) for relatively minor matters, believing that the fees will be less. If you elect to move to a smaller organization, you should determine what that will do to your client base, present and potential—diminish it or enlarge it. Bear in mind that many smaller firms compete successfully for major matters against their larger Wall Street rivals.

Moving from the Small Firm to the Large Firm

The lawyer in the small firm may decide that he or she no longer wants the burden of keeping abreast of developments in a variety of disciplines and would prefer to specialize in one area, while having the resources of a large firm to provide the expertise he or she lacks.

In both these situations, the lawyer with experience may be able to find a firm with a need that can be filled. Locating the right opportunity may require that you make a diligent effort: Make your availability known to search firms specializing in helping lawyers, by direct contacts with partners in target firms, and by networking with fellow lawyers to let them know that you are looking for a change.

For the older lawyer, either contemplating or having reached retirement, the shift in firms can be traumatic. If one has a client base that will remain productive, a target firm will find it much easier to make an offer. If the client base is diminishing, a new firm is less likely to commit office space and services for an of counsel or similar arrangement. Moreover, the older lawyer must recognize that, with rare exceptions, it is more difficult to expand one's list of clients after age sixty-five than it is at an earlier age.

This suggests that if you are on the verge of retirement and contemplating a move to another firm, you might reconsider and think about staying on in an of counsel capacity. There are obvious advantages. Your clients know the firm and are probably comfortable in dealing with you as part of that organization. Also, your name (we will assume) has been associated with that firm for a substantial period of time. Should you leave that firm, you lose the value of that association. Your clients and potential clients may not even remember the name of your new firm, and you may lose business as a result. It is also true that if you have had a long association with one firm, you have grown to know your fellow lawyers and to understand their idiosyncrasies. Were you to join another firm, you will need time to become familiar with their foibles. To stay where you are avoids the stress that comes with change.

Whether you choose to stay with your present firm or to accept an of counsel position elsewhere, there should be a written agreement to govern your postretirement employment. The nature and content of that agreement will be discussed in Chapter 6.

Opening Your Own Office

If you have finally come to the realization that neither the large nor the small law firm has any appeal, but you want to remain in law practice, there is only one course open to you: hanging out your shingle as a single practitioner or forming a new law office in conjunction with other lawyers in a similar situation. Here again, age is a factor. It is usually easier for the younger lawyer to take this plunge. However, younger lawyers often have burdens, financial or family or both, that do not permit it. For the older lawyer, it is a feasible alternative if the move is made soon enough to allow for building of a client base—I would say before age sixty—unless, of course, one has sufficient financial resources so that there is no pressing necessity to obtain clients.

One advantage to be considered, should you elect to join with others in establishing a law office, is a sharing of costs. Some of the items of expense to be discussed below can be split among the participants, resulting in a lowering of overhead. Put another way, the same expenditure of funds may enable all participants to have the benefit of nicer surroundings.

Costs to Open Your Office

The expense involved in opening an office is a major consideration for most practitioners. The section that follows sets forth a general discussion of the capital and operating costs involved in "hanging out a shingle." It also presents a list of items that need to be considered by anyone contemplating opening a law office. Following the discussion are two examples of the costs one might encounter in opening either a modest office in a small city or rural town having low rent and clerical support salaries or a more upscale office in a larger community.

Malpractice Insurance

The premium for malpractice insurance is a major item of cost for any legal practitioner. The factors determining what you will have to pay are discussed in Chapter 3. As noted there, premiums are based on a number of considerations, including the type of practice, the level of experience of the attorney, and the area of the country. Before you can obtain a definitive cost figure, you may be obliged to file an extensive application form with a carrier or carriers serving your area.

Furniture

The furniture needs of an office may seem obvious and hardly worth mentioning, but for the sake of jogging your awareness, we will review them: a desk and chairs for you and your secretary, a credenza or work table for you, a bookcase, file cabinets, reception room table and chairs, appropriate lamps, and floor coverings. By purchasing economically (you might even consider buying second-hand furniture), you could probably acquire these basic items for as little as $2,000. Any betterment, even in a modest office, will put your expenditures up toward $10,000. And in the upscale office, furniture costs will run at least $20,000.

Furniture requirements vary according to type of practice and personal idiosyncrasies, including the types of equipment being used in the office. An attorney who is not computer-literate will not have a personal computer, for instance. However, this attorney may need dictating equipment (and a secretary who knows how to use it) and a place to put it. An attorney who uses the computer a great deal may want a special computer desk to facilitate use of the equipment.

Equipment

In today's world, even a small law office must be technologically up-to-date. You will need a computer, modem, printer, copier, fax machine, word processing software, accounting software, interconnection software, and a telephone system. All of this can be purchased for under $5,000. If you are computer-literate, you may need an extra personal computer in your office, which may add another $3,000 to your budget.

Supplies

Initially, you will have to stock your office with such items as stationery, computer paper, copier paper, fax paper, legal pads, file folders, computer diskettes and file boxes, and such mechanical devices as calculators and staplers. Then there is a myriad of miscellaneous items, none of which are individually expensive but which add up in the aggregate. Count on spending about $1,500 for these things.

Total

The capital investment for your office will run at least $3,500 for a modest office and not less than $12,000 for something a little better, but by no means elaborate. Should you have a fancy for Oriental rugs or Chinese period art, the sky is the limit. If you have a friend in the used furniture business, you may be able to reduce these figures substantially.

There is also the alternative of renting much of the office equipment, thus saving the loss of capital you otherwise would suffer if you chose to purchase instead.

The capital costs discussed thus far do not include the cost of renting an office. The landlord may want a security deposit, and if you are not comfortable with the local real estate law and customs, you may choose to hire a real estate lawyer to handle your lease negotiations. These items could add another $1,500 to $3,000 to your investment.

In short, to be safe, you need to have between $10,000 and $15,000 available to hang out your shingle. You may also want to add a cushion to absorb operating costs for several months until you can generate some business, send out some bills, and have some receipts from which to meet your office overhead and cover your personal expenses.

Depending upon your location, the size and configuration of your residence, and the willingness of your spouse to put up with your working arrangement, there is always the possibility of establishing an office in your home. The saving in going this route is in rent and utilities. Check the local zoning regulations to be sure that an office in your home will not constitute a violation. Many utility providers offer help to the person organizing a home office. For example, the New York Telephone Company offers a booklet on "Instant Help for the Home Office: 8 Ways to Work Smarter from Home." A copy is available without charge from the Home Office Center, P.O. Box 4106, Huntington Station, NY 11746-9250.

Whether or not an office in your home is practical depends upon other factors as well. A home office may fail to attract—or may even dissuade—certain types of clients and their business. If the home is not in a commercial area, and most homes are not, there is the question of projecting a suitable image. It may be difficult for prospective clients to find your office; and they may feel a lack of privacy in coming to your home, particularly if you and the client are both well known in your community and to your neighbors. There are difficult problems in satisfying the tax authorities as to the legitimacy of write-offs of practice-related expenses. If you study these problems and resolve them to your satisfaction, then a home office may be an answer for you.

Operating Costs

Once you have opened the door, you need to think about the costs of operating the office. Some are fairly obvious: rent, utilities, and maintenance; clerical salary, Social Security, and medical insurance costs; renter's insurance; and telephone.

Clerical assistance may cost more than you think. Most attorneys today do their own "typing" work on a personal computer. The "secretary" does bookkeeping, billing, and filing, and also makes appointments for the attorney and attends to reception of clients. He or she must be a "jack of all trades." And it goes without saying that an unqualified "secretary" is a menace to one's practice. Consequently, you can expect that the salary for a well-qualified individual may be above the going rate for an average office worker.

An item of operating costs not listed or discussed here is an automobile. If you can use your car in your practice, you may be able to charge some of its related expense to client matters and charge some unreimbursed expense as a tax deduction.

The operating costs of a practice are in addition to costs that are charged directly to clients. Normally, an office charges clients for unusual postage, copier usage, facsimile dispatch and receipt, telephone toll and long distance charges, and travel expense. Some offices may charge for other items as well. Clients sometimes refuse or fail to pay—or are charged insufficient amounts to cover—these costs. Your budget must take this into account. (This is one of the assumptions in the tables on pages 64 and 65 of this chapter.)

Then there are the costs that are not so evident, such as subscriptions, library and Lexis or Westlaw fees, and professional dues.

Most law offices subscribe to one or more legal newspapers or magazines, just to keep up with what is going on in the profession. You will probably also want to subscribe to some legal treatises or reviews. Perhaps you would be subscribing to these whether or not you opened your own office, but you mustn't forget that they are a cost.

You will need a library to cover the basics in your area of practice. If you are fortunate, you will be able to locate your office near a well-maintained law library available, perhaps, on a membership fee basis, which is much less expensive than trying to keep your own library stocked and up-to-date. Your local bar association may have an adequate library. Depending upon the coverage from the combination of your own volumes and those in the library, you can decide whether you need to have the services of Lexis or Westlaw available in your office. Usually, the monthly on-line cost is in the vicinity of $125, although local bar associations sometimes offer a monthly on-line opportunity for as little as $25, with connect-time at an additional charge. The connect-time charges can usually be passed on to the client for whom they were incurred, unless you have a person who objects to paying for services except on an all-inclusive fee basis.

You must also remember whether or not your lease covers utility charges. If it does not, they are a monthly expense. Your landlord may also expect you to hire and supervise the daily cleaning and routine maintenance of your office. In some buildings, the landlord reserves the right to choose and hire the cleaning contractor, but you are committed to payment of a pro rata portion of the contractor's charge. This is an operating cost you should determine and figure in your operating budget. The telephone bill can also be substantial, depending on the circumstances of your practice. If you expect to have a considerable amount of on-line time with Lexis/Nexis or Westlaw, you have to figure that as a charge additional to what you would anticipate from use of your telephone only for conversation.

A few years ago, one never considered advertising to be an expense item for a law office. But as we all know, that has now changed. Marketing—or advertising—costs appear in the budgets of practically every law firm these days. Your practice will probably be no exception. Whether you advertise in legal journals, in the local press, or on radio or television, you need to have a budget for these costs and be prepared to absorb them. Think about what sort of advertising you plan to do and then investigate the costs, so that your budget is realistic. The possibilities are endless, and it would serve little purpose to discuss here the costs associated with any particular medium. Advertising is discretionary, and although it is used by most law firms in one form or another (it goes under the headings of "marketing" or "client development"), if you choose, you can spend nothing on this sort of expense.

All equipment, including office equipment, has a tendency to break down. You may have a service contract with your supplier, or you may elect to handle the repairs as they arise. In any event, figure something in your budget to cover the cost of equipment repair. Bear in mind that modern office equipment is technically sophisticated and requires repair technicians with substantial knowledge. Their hourly rates are high and their bills are commensurate with their hourly rates. Don't underestimate what you will have to pay for technical repairs. To avoid the unexpected, you might consider renting, rather than purchasing, some of the more sophisticated equipment, and under terms that require the lessor to make repairs or replace a machine if necessary.

As your practice develops and you write more letters, prepare numerous reports, and receive lots of faxes, you will find that your supplies have begun to dwindle. Naturally, they will have to be replaced; so you need to include in your operating budget the cost of replacing those office supplies that were included in your original investment but are being consumed in your practice.

Setting Your Rate

There are two methods of establishing an hourly rate for your services: (1) Estimate what you believe is the going rate, i.e., what your competition is charging, and use that as your own rate, or (2) decide what you want to bring in as *gross* income and divide that number by the hours you expect to be able to *bill*.

The first method is fraught with problems. If you underestimate the going rate, you are cheating yourself and, perhaps, demeaning yourself in the eyes of your potential clients; if you overestimate, you will lose clients.

The second method is more difficult to implement. The amount of gross income required is a function of adding your contemplated operating expense and the take-home pay you wish to award yourself. The validity of this determination rests on accuracy in estimating expenses. Once the amount of gross income is established, you must then calculate how many hours you expect to bill during the year. Here, again, you must take into account not only the obvious lost days (and hours) but those less apparent: time required to attend to administrative details of your office, in filing required reports with various supervisory agencies in your jurisdiction, in completing tax returns, in client development efforts such as luncheon functions and so forth. Dividing gross income by true billable hours provides the rate you must charge your clients. Once this is done, you have only one remaining problem: getting the clients in the door!

Executive Office Service Facilities
In many locations, services provide, in an agreeable setting, office facilities for executives and professional people, usually on a transient basis; that is, the rental is for a relatively brief period. The service provides an individual office, receptionist, conference rooms, telephone and facsimile services, photocopier, and sometimes filing and billing services. While using a service can be considerably less expensive than opening one's own individual office, for the lawyer it presents difficulties in ensuring that there is no violation of the Model Rules of Professional Responsibility.

When lawyers practice together, the knowledge of any one lawyer respecting a client's matter is imputed to all others in the office for conflicts purposes. Even when they do not practice together but have access to each other's files, the same rule applies. Therefore, the lawyer who takes space in an executive service facility where there are other lawyers present must be certain that none of the other lawyers have access to his files and that he does not discuss any of his clients' matters with the other attorneys.

The lawyer also has an obligation to ensure confidentiality of communications with clients. In an executive service facility, employees of the facility might have access to clients' information and communications that are supposed to remain confidential. These employees are not employees of the lawyer who, in the lawyer's own office, would be entitled to have access to such information and communications. To ensure proper treatment of clients' matters, the lawyer would have to be certain that only he or she would handle documents and communications entitled to confidentiality.

Some attorneys using executive office services have been able to deal with the ethical issues satisfactorily. First, they make sure that their files are accessible only to themselves and are kept under lock and key when they are not present in the suite. Similarly, they have a desk in a separate room that can be locked when the lawyer is not present, in order to protect the confidentiality of any client papers. The support staff of the suite is instructed regarding confidentiality, much as one would instruct the support staff of a law firm; given their limited contact with the client's matters, with great care the ethical problem can probably be avoided.

Two Examples of Capital and Operating Costs

The estimated annual costs to set up and operate a law office under two different sets of circumstances are shown in the tables on pages 64 and 65. Obviously, the costs to establish and operate an upscale office are higher. But whatever the costs, they relate to the hourly rate that you must charge to obtain the income you need, assuming that you will have sufficient business to keep busy for the number of hours projected in your forecast. In each of our examples, we assume that the lawyer will be able to bill 1,600 hours per year. Unless you have the work to fill those hours and can bill clients for them, the cost and earnings estimates will have no validity.

As we have stated, many factors affect costs. The area of the country bears on the amount that must be spent for malpractice insurance premiums, rent, and clerical support. The type of practice will also bear upon malpractice insurance premiums and the kind of office one will need to properly service the type of client the practice will attract.

One example shows the possible capital and operating costs you might encounter in setting up an office in a small city or rural town, with lower costs for rent and clerical support services and no legal services contemplated that would require an upgraded malpractice insurance premium. The second example is for a more upscale office in a larger community where rents are higher and clerical costs greater. This office might support more sophisticated legal work involving a higher malpractice insurance premium.

As you review the assumptions below, bear in mind that in the larger cities operating costs can be expected to be somewhat higher than one may expect in the rest of the country.

Assumptions: Modest Office

The modest office, in terms of usable space, might contain approximately 425 square feet (sq ft); i.e., a small reception area of

100 sq ft, secretary's office of 100 sq ft, and an attorney's office of 225 sq ft. Rental is calculated at $10/sq ft per annum. The office has one secretary and a single computer, copier, and fax machine, which are rented, as is the telephone equipment. Legal research services are supplied by computer from a national publisher.

Assumptions: Upscale Office

The upscale office suggests usable space of approximately 1,775 sq ft (i.e., reception area, 500 sq ft; conference room, 750 sq ft; secretary's office, 225 sq ft; and attorney's office, 300 sq ft) in a somewhat better class of office building than the modest office. Rental would be $25/sq ft per annum. The secretarial function would be performed by one full-time and one part-time secretary. The office would have two computer terminals and a better grade of copier and fax machine, all on rental. Telephone equipment would be slightly more sophisticated and more expensive than in the modest office. Legal services in "hard copy" would be more expensive and would supplement the computer-provided product, but would be furnished by a national service.

Equipment Rental vs. Purchase

Some lawyers might be averse to rental of office equipment and might prefer to purchase whatever is required. We show two scenarios, one for the modest office and another for the upscale office, with office machinery being purchased.

The modest office would have a single computer terminal with monitor, a modem, and a small laser printer; a modest copier; a single fax machine; and a typewriter (or word processor), which is useful for addressing envelopes and making labels. The office would have a single file cabinet and a computer table or station for the secretary's office.

The upscale office would have two personal computers, but only one would be equipped with an internal modem. This office would have a faster laser printer than the more modest office. Its copier would have reduction and enlargement capability. The office would have a single fax machine and a single word processor. It would have two file cabinets. There would be a computer table in the attorney's office and a computer work station in the secretary's office.

ANNUAL COSTS TO SET UP AND OPERATE A LAW OFFICE

	Modest Office	Upscale Office
Costs Based on Equipment Rental		
CAPITAL COSTS		
Furniture for		
Reception room	$ 900	$ 3,500
Secretary	300	1,750
Conference room	n/a	1,750
Initial supplies	1,500	2,000
Attorney	800	3,000
Total capital costs	$3,500	$12,000
OPERATING COSTS—Based on rental of office machinery		
Rent	$ 4,250	$ 44,375
Malpractice insurance	2,400	8,500
Secretarial service and benefits	18,000	25,000
Occupational fees and dues	800	1,200
Utilities (heat, light, water)	1,600	6,500
Computer rental w/software	3,600	7,000
Copier rental	1,200	1,500
Fax rental	600	800
Legal services	3,200	6,000
Miscellaneous items		
(office supplies, postage, etc.)	3,000	6,000
Telephone	2,400	3,500
Total operating costs	$41,050	$110,375

By making such purchases, the lawyer, although increasing the capital cost required to establish the office, would eliminate the related equipment rental cost from the annual office operating costs. Thus, for the modest office, the capital outlay would rise to $7,700; and for the upscale office, to $21,100. At the same time, annual operating costs would be reduced by $5,400, to $35,650, for the modest office and by $9,300 to $101,075, for the upscale office.

The savings of operating costs in the modest office of $5,400 annually should be equated against the loss of return on the investment of $4,200 and the fact that computer hardware tends to become obsolete in as brief a period as three years; assuming a

ANNUAL COSTS TO SET UP AND OPERATE A LAW OFFICE, *continued*

	Modest Office	Upscale Office
Costs Based on Equipment Purchase		
ADDITIONAL CAPITAL COSTS		
Computer(s)	$1,650	$3,750
Software	500	1,000
Modem	75	75
Printer	500	1,350
Copier	400	1,500
Fax machine	400	400
Typewriter	300	500
File cabinet(s)	150	300
Computer table(s)	225	225
Total	$4,200	$9,100
Calculation of Hourly Rate		
ANNUAL EXPENSES		
Interest on additional capital costs at 9%	$ 375	$ 820
Operating costs	41,050	110,375
Income requirement before taxes	50,000	125,000
Total	$91,425	$236,195
APPROXIMATE HOURLY RATE		
Required to cover costs plus income desired	$60	$150

total pretax return of 9 percent and obsolescence in three years, the annual savings of $5,400 must be reduced by about $1,400 to $3,600 to find a net figure. In the case of the upscale office, the savings of $9,300 would be reduced by some $3,100 to $5,850 per annum to achieve a net figure. The $1,400 and the $3,100, respectively, represent the amount you should set aside, or reserve, each year in order to replace your equipment at the end of its useful life.

Despite the fact that rental charges for computer equipment are quite high (not unexpected, given the equipment's short life) and notwithstanding the necessity for a high reserve, it may nonetheless be desirable to rent rather than purchase, provided that the lease is short-term; you can then secure new equipment at the end of the lease term. If the lessor is willing to replace the hardware at short, stipulated intervals, a longer-term lease may be acceptable. Frequent replacement assures that the office will always have up-to-date machinery. The bottom line is that the difference in net cost between purchasing and leasing is not significant.

Based upon these capital and operating costs, one may calculate (a) how many hours one must bill and (b) at what rate, in order to earn a specified income. For example, let us suppose that the lawyer in the modest office is content to earn $50,000 before taxes, while the lawyer in the more upscale office would anticipate an income of $125,000 before taxes. We have provided the calculations to show that their approximate hourly rates would have to be $60 and $150, respectively.

If equipment is purchased rather than rented, there is little effect upon the hourly rate the lawyer must charge. Based on the numbers in our examples, purchasing would enable only an insignificant hourly charge reduction in the range of $1 to $3.

Finally, a comment about setting an hourly rate is in order. If you decide to hang out your shingle, you are probably aware of the highly competitive atmosphere in which you will practice. Today, clients, particularly business clients, are looking for a deal. Business itself is highly competitive, and everyone in business is searching for ways to keep costs lower than the competitors' costs; lowering the outlays for legal service is one step toward that goal. You may be asked to give a discount from your "usual" hourly rate, to offer a package of services for a single fee, or to provide a volume discount. A few years ago, most lawyers would have been horrified at that prospect. Today, none can afford that luxury. You, too, must be prepared to adapt to the times.

Establishing a Real Estate Practice*

Practically every senior citizen is faced with considering alternative living arrangements. The only real question is how soon the move will be made and to what place. A senior citizen—in fact,

*The author is indebted to Stanley B. Balbach, Esq., and Edward T. Flynn, Esq., both of Illinois, for their contributions to this section.

any person, senior or not, making such a change—needs independent legal advice in considering living alternatives.

The largest financial transaction that an individual is likely to have in a lifetime is the purchase or sale of a home. This is particularly true of a senior citizen whose entire estate, with the exception of retirement benefits, may consist of home equity. This offers senior lawyers an opportunity for a second career in advising seniors who need advice in these matters. The senior lawyers are thus provided with an opportunity to supplement their retirement incomes.

Senior lawyers who have not practiced in the area of real estate law, and who decide upon a career change in this direction, may be concerned that they lack the knowledge to function correctly and effectively. Most bar associations and professional organizations from time to time offer courses in their continuing legal education series that will provide the senior lawyer with an appropriate level of "retreading."

Quite apart from discussing pure real estate issues, serving as counselor to seniors ready to make a change in housing can offer a tremendous opportunity for the senior lawyer to be of help. For example, consider the family of seniors contemplating the sale of a home where they have lived for a number of years. The first and most obvious question that you, as their lawyer, should ask is, "Why do these people want to sell?" While this may not be a legal question, the answer may reveal, not only to you but especially to them, many other practical problems. By virtue of your age and experience, you may be in an advantageous position to help solve them.

The seniors may advance various reasons to justify their decision. Should you elect to pursue a second career as a real estate lawyer, you may have the opportunity to ask some searching questions; the answers your clients give themselves may help them avoid disastrous decisions and provide you with enormous satisfaction.

A DIFFERENT CLIMATE. Seniors may suggest to you that they would like to live in a more favorable climate. You may ask whether they have tried living in the climate of their choice. Arizona, Florida, and southern California may seem much different in the summer than in the winter. Colorado, Wyoming, the upper peninsula of Michigan, and the Maine coast may be delightful in the summer, but have these seniors tried living there in the winter? You might suggest that the investment in spending a full year in the contemplated climate is modest compared with the cost if they make a permanent move and are unhappy with their choice.

CLOSER TO FAMILY. This reason needs careful analysis as well. When seniors move to an area in order to join adult children, it presents a host of different problems. While some or none may ever arise, the potential is always there: One of the children may receive a promotion and be obliged to transfer to another distant location; perhaps the spouse of a child will be less than thrilled to have the in-laws so close by. A thorough test of proximity is a good recommendation to make.

A RETIREMENT HOME. Should your clients suggest moving to a retirement home, you might propose that, before purchasing space—a room or an apartment—they test living in that facility, possibly through a rental arrangement, but at minimum they should visit the facility extensively.

RETURN TO A FAMILY HOME OR FARM. Life at the "old place" was one thing when your clients were youngsters growing up. Things may have changed dramatically over the years, particularly in the neighborhood or other environment. Before they make such a shift, you might suggest to your clients that they test out the move by returning on a temporary basis.

A SHORTAGE OF FUNDS. Should your clients' income be insufficient to care for them adequately, or should they wish to improve their life-style modestly, you could think about recommending that they obtain a "reverse mortgage." The basic concept is the transfer of title to your clients' home to a lender; the lender then pays the transferor a sum monthly for as long as your clients continue to live in the house. The concept of reverse mortgages is still in a formative stage. While many such "loans" have been made in California, they remain uncommon elsewhere—and in many places are simply not available. Some reverse mortgages provide for lifetime payments to the owner as long as the home is occupied by the original owners, and others have time and other limitations. A full discussion of the mechanics of reverse mortgages is beyond the scope of this book. A further description is contained in *The Lawyer's Guide to Retirement*, edited by David A. Bridewell, originally published by the ABA Senior Lawyers Division in 1991, with a revised edition available early in 1994. The American Association of Retired Persons may also be able to furnish additional information.

All of your clients' plans for relocation, except for the matter of a reverse mortgage, involve the sale of their home. It is important in such a sale that they have independent legal advice. The first thought of many prospective sellers is to talk to their friendly real estate broker. This course can be followed if they recognize that the broker is only *partially* on their team. The broker is interested in earning the largest commission possible in the shortest length of time. The seller wants the best price available, which may mean a different pricing structure and a different offering time than favored by the broker. The advertising by the broker, the methods of showing the house, the duration of the listing agreement, and the broker's personal commitment are all matters that need to be negotiated.

Many seniors have had experience during their lifetimes in buying and selling residential property; but many others have not, and those who have are often unaware of which arrangements are customary and fixed and which are negotiable. Since there usually is at stake such a substantial portion of your clients' resources, you can be of help, as a real estate lawyer, in negotiating an agreement with the broker that is in the best interest of the sellers. You may be able to assure that the contract is clear as to when a commission is earned and in what amount. You can obtain minimum advertising commitments and include them in the contract. You can provide for the system of notification to the sellers when brokers wish to show the property. You may be able to talk with several brokers and make an arrangement with the one who offers the most advantageous arrangement at the lowest commission rate.

Once the property is sold and, as the sellers' attorney, you have the reponsibility of preparing the contract, you have an opportunity to be of substantial assistance to your clients in ensuring that they do not purchase another property until the contingencies in their contract of sale have been satisfied, and that there is ample time after the contingencies have been met and the closing date to allow them to acquire another home. You may be able to assist them in obtaining a "bridge loan" to provide funds between the closing date on their old home and the closing date on their new home, so that they can make the transition smoothly.

When the seniors who are your clients are buyers, then you should be sure that you obtain from them their understanding of what the seller's terms should be. You may find that their understanding of their deal with the seller is quite different from the terms in the document prepared and presented by the seller. Indeed, in some parts of the country, the real estate broker is on both sides of the transaction. This might appear to offer some protection to the buyer, but frequently the buyer's broker is paid part of the commission negotiated by the seller, thus limiting the economic protection.

In the process of advising seniors and others in residential real estate transactions, you will find a great deal of second-career satisfaction. The lawyer is the only available advisor who does not have a conflict. The real estate broker wants the highest commission, payable as soon as possible, with the easiest contract terms so that the property will sell rapidly. The lender desires the highest interest rate with the least hassle in regard to the terms of the loan, resulting in a product that can be readily sold on the secondary mortgage market. The buyer is in conflict with the broker as to the amount of the down payment, purchase price, date of possession, apportionment of insurance, and designation of includable and excludable personal property. Bear in mind that if the seller's broker is not the selling broker, the buyer's broker having arranged the actual sale, the buyer's broker may be oriented toward the buyer. However, the seller's broker does not want to lose a part of the commission. The protection of the seller in these circumstances must come through the seller's lawyer, because he or she will be paid whether or not the sale is concluded and therefore has no conflict.

Home buyers and sellers—and particularly senior citizens who have so much at stake—need the benefit of independent legal counsel prior to the time a decision is made to sell their home, hire a broker, move to an attractive climate, negotiate a reverse mortage, or move into a retirement home.

The lawyer who is retired—whether from a law firm, the military, a corporate legal department, a judgeship, or other legal career—who desires a career in real estate law practice, but lacks training in the handling of real estate transactions, will find training available. Law schools, title insurance companies (commercial and bar-related), junior colleges, and universities offer courses. A second career in real estate is a natural outlet for a senior lawyer because friends and acquaintances are likely to be of an age when a change of residence is a likely and important step. But if it is not considered and planned carefully, this step can be disastrous.

Real Estate Brokerage

Still another possibility is work as a real estate broker or agent. In some states, such as New York, a person who is licensed as an attorney-at-law may legally receive a sales commission in a real estate transaction; a separate license is not necessary. Should you wish to pursue a more leisurely life-style, consider real estate sales on either a full- or part-time basis.

However, before making a commitment, be sure you check into the customs of the real estate offices in your area and be sure you find nothing to surprise or upset you. For example, in some areas of the country, the individual agent—not the agency—is responsible for the cost of advertising a property. It is also important to inform as many people as possible that you are now in this business, because when a property is sold, if you can be the "listing broker," your share of the sales commission will be greater. You also need to be sure that your car is presentable and suitable for taking prospects to view properties.

Getting started and establishing a foothold in the industry can require considerable cash outlays. You need to be sure that you have the necessary resources for advertising, for the significant cost associated with mailing of your notices, and for automobile maintenance and operation.

Because of the inherent conflicts mentioned above in our discussion of a second career as a real estate lawyer, it is probably inadvisable to try to serve as both a real estate broker and also as a real estate lawyer. There is satisfaction in doing either job well. Choose the one that better suits your personality and aspirations.

6

Drafting the Of Counsel Agreement

As the lawyer approaches the age when retirement is inevitable, he or she needs to think about the modus vivendi once that day arrives. What a person wants to do after retirement, how much work is desired, how much work will be permitted, the nature of the relationship, the amount of compensation, if any—all these factors will dictate the type of arrangement and the type of agreement that will evolve.

Partners' Agreements and Restrictions on Competition

Before a lawyer who is a member of a law firm is able to conclude what he or she will do upon retirement, he or she needs to know what the firm will permit him or her to do. Consequently, if you are a law firm partner, read carefully the partners' agreement that governs your firm and note those provisions affecting the ability of the firm to compel retirement, any scaledown of compensation before retirement, practice of law after retirement, duties toward the firm after retirement, compensation for services, and benefits obtainable. In this connection, a word of caution: Some partnership agreements may attempt to restrict the right of the retiree to compete with the firm. However, under the Model Rules of Professional Conduct 5.6, the firm may restrict the competition of the partner only during a period when the firm is actually making payments to the retiree.

Government and Corporate Lawyers

Lawyers who are in government service should be aware of the federal or state statutes, as the case may be, that govern the activities of employees who have left government, and should be aware of any court decisions interpreting these statutes. Lawyers on corporate payrolls should check their own personnel files to ensure that the employment arrangements with the corporation do not contain any restriction as to the type of work a retired employee may pursue after retirement, particularly as it may relate to representing entities in competition with the corporation.

Now, let us assume that you are in a partnership and that you have read the partnership agreement. It contains nothing earth-shattering, but on the other hand, it leaves unanswered a number of questions regarding your rights, responsibilities, and benefits after retirement. What should you do?

The Written Agreement

The obvious answer would seem to be to have a written agreement. Unfortunately, many firms do not have a separate agreement with their retired partners. This can lead to confusion and misunderstanding. You, as the retiree, have the greatest interest in avoiding this situation. You should press for that separate agreement. And, if you are joining an organization with which you have no prior affiliation, it is equally important—for somewhat different reasons—that you have a written agreement.

What should the agreement contain?

Nature of the Relationship

First, it is important to decide what type of relationship you want to have with your firm. Do you want to be an employee or an independent contractor? The answer to this question may have a number of consequences, such as the effect on your taxes, your health and disability insurance protection, and your independence in your activities. Because of these factors, you may want to be an employee for some purposes and an independent contractor for others.

USE OF TITLE "OF COUNSEL" (OPINION 90-357)

No matter which relationship you have, you probably will be called "of counsel" or "counsel" or some similar title. Because of Formal Opinion No. 90-357 of the ABA Standing Committee on Ethics and Professional Responsibility issued on May 10, 1990 (herein "Opinion 90-357"), there are both requirements and limits with respect to use of the title "of counsel."

What about use of the title? The caption to Opinion 90-357 states it succinctly:

> The use of the title "of counsel," or variants of that title, in identifying the relationship of a lawyer or law firm with another lawyer or firm is permissible as long as the relationship between the two is a close, regular, personal relationship and the use of the title is not otherwise false or misleading.

AVOIDANCE OF LIABILITY

But apart from title, there are other reasons to be clear in defining the relationship with your firm. Certainly, you want to avoid having the liability of a partner, so you must avoid the indicia of partnership. The doctrine of apparent authority applies here.

EMPLOYEE OR INDEPENDENT CONTRACTOR

Before you start drafting an of counsel agreement, you have to ask yourself, and answer, a number of questions. Do you want to be an employee of the firm or an independent contractor? If you are an employee, there are certain advantages: As an employee, you are entitled to fringe benefits, such as medical and disability insurance; usually, as an employee, you will have no minimum hours. And there is a disadvantage: As an employee, you cannot report your unreimbursed expenses on Schedule C but must report them on Schedule A, and will thus be subject to the 2 percent floor on miscellaneous deductions; that is, the only unreimbursed expenses you can deduct are those exceeding 2 percent of adjusted gross income.

If you are an independent contractor, you will not be controlled in your activities, as you would be if you were an employee. You can deduct your unreimbursed expenses without being subject to the 2 percent floor. However, as Harold Wren points out in his article "How to Structure Of Counsel for Tax Advantage," which appeared in the Spring 1993 edition of *Experience* magazine, as an independent contractor, you may have to pay only one-half of the 15.3 percent Social Security tax. (In 1993, this tax applied on the first $57,100 of income.) This is so because the independent contractor is permitted an adjustment of one-half the tax in the "adjustments" section of Form 1040 (currently on Line 25), so that filing in that capacity cuts in half the amount that must be paid. The independent contractor, therefore, receives the same tax treatment for the Social Security tax as an employee. Nevertheless, as an independent contractor you might be excluded from medical and disability benefits that apply only to employees and not to independent contractors.

Your safest bet is to choose the best of all worlds: Establish yourself as an independent contractor for purposes of your relationship with your firm, but commit the firm to treating you as an employee for purposes of malpractice insurance, health insurance, and other benefit plans.

What do you need to do to establish your relationship, for tax purposes, as an independent contractor? Mr. Wren, in his article, sets out a litany of questions. He states that, "If some of the following questions are answered in the affirmative, the relationship is that of an employer-employee; if not, then the parties are independent contractors."

Here is Mr. Wren's list:

1. Must the lawyer comply with the firm's instructions regarding his or her work?
2. Does the lawyer receive training from or at the direction of the firm?
3. Does the lawyer provide services that are integrated into the firm's business?
4. Does the lawyer provide services that must be rendered personally?
5. Is the lawyer precluded from hiring, supervising, or paying assistants for the firm?

6. Does the lawyer have a continuing relationship with the firm?
7. Must the lawyer follow set hours of work?
8. Does the lawyer work full time for the firm?
9. Does the lawyer work in the firm's office?
10. Must the lawyer work in a sequence set by the firm?
11. Must the lawyer submit regular reports to the firm?
12. Does the lawyer receive regular payments at set intervals?
13. Does the lawyer receive payments for business or traveling expenses?
14. Does the lawyer rely on the firm to furnish tools and materials?
15. Does the lawyer lack a major investment in the facilities used to perform his or her services?
16. Is the arrangement such that the lawyer cannot make a profit or suffer a loss from his or her services?
17. Does the lawyer work for one firm at a time?
18. Is the arrangement such that the lawyer does not offer his or her services to the general public?
19. May the lawyer be fired by the firm?
20. May the lawyer quit work at any time without incurring liability?

Note that, as Mr. Wren states, you do not need to answer all of these questions in the affirmative to be classified as an employee.

In any event, whether employee or independent contractor, it is important that you think about malpractice insurance and plan to include in the agreement the understanding between you and your firm as to whether as of counsel you will be covered. Malpractice policies are "claims made" policies. Consequently, policies that may have covered you before retirement no longer cover you thereafter, unless you have a specific agreement with your former firm. And, as we noted in the discussion in Chapter 3, premiums are high. Rightly or wrongly, the carriers take the position that the more experienced the lawyer, the more complicated and sophisticated are the transactions he undertakes and thus there is a greater risk of substantial exposure to the carrier. Up go the premiums.

Duties as Of Counsel

The of counsel agreement should spell out the nature and extent of your duties. Will you have responsibilities to clients and, if so, exactly how will they change, if at all, from your responsibilities as a partner? Will you be required to turn over responsibility for your clients to other partners in the firm? Will you be required or permitted to perform legal services, either for your old clients, for new clients you have obtained, or for other clients of the firm? Will you have any administrative duties? Will you be permitted to attend firm meetings? Will you be required or permitted to serve on firm committees? Will you have any client development obligations? Will you have any obligation to assist in the hiring or training of new lawyers for the firm?

The importance of spelling out which duties of counsel is to perform cannot be overemphasized. If you, as of counsel, are to have the benefits of various benefit programs that accrue only to persons active in the firm, then you must expect to have responsibilities which you must discharge. And certain medical programs permit enrollment of only those persons who work a minimum number of hours, usually about thirty, per week. Some duties are therefore in your best interest.

You will have to juggle between those provisions that assure your status as an independent contractor and those which may make you an employee. The better course would seem to be to aim for those creating independent contractor status and then to add provisions in your agreement providing the malpractice protection and medical and insurance benefits that you desire and the firm is willing to provide.

Requirements for Title

Opinion 90-357 does not permit the use of the title of counsel in the situation where the lawyer is affiliated only for a single case, although it seems permissible to list a lawyer or firm as of counsel in the pleadings, where it is clear that the relationship pertains only to that particular case. The title may not apply for "casual collaborative efforts," or where the relationship is that of an outside consultant. Bear in mind that Opinion 90-357 requires that the relationship must be close, regular, and personal; the assignment of duties should reflect that situation.

In New York, according to a Nassau County ethics opinion, a lawyer may affiliate as of counsel to two law firms; but in Ohio, for example, the same lawyer may not practice law as of counsel with more than one law firm at one time. Also in New York, according to a Nassau County opinion, a lawyer may not be designated as of counsel when his or her sole function is the referral of clients to the firm. Use of the title must involve the performance of legal services by the lawyer. Fee splitting is not permitted. Just to show that you must look at the local rules in the state where you might plan to serve, note that in Arizona a firm can split fees with its of counsel lawyer if it does so on the basis of the amount of work done by the firm and the lawyer. However, in Texas, fee splitting is permitted with the of counsel who has a regular, continuing, and substantial relationship with the firm. In March 1993, the Los Angeles County Bar Association issued Ethics Opinion No. 470, which declares that payment of a year-end bonus to an of counsel attorney "who is not a partner, associate, or shareholder of the law firm" as a percentage of the profits derived from the business referred to the firm from the attorney is prohibited; it states that, without client consent, the payment would violate California Rule 2-200 banning fee splitting.

Second Careers

Not every of counsel is a lawyer retired from a law firm. Often of counsel is on a second career, perhaps a person retired from a corporation or from government or from the educational world. The working standards in each of these institutions vary greatly from each other and from those of most law firms. To avoid misunderstandings during the course of the new relationship, it is important that the duties of "second career" people be described clearly and adequately.

The Firm's Responsibilities

The firm should have certain duties toward you, and these should be spelled out. Must the firm provide you with an office?

Of what size? What office services are to be available to you, and will you be obliged to pay for any of these services or will they be provided at no charge to you? Will the firm pay or reimburse you for dues to, or expenses in attending meetings of, professional organizations, and if so, which entities? Will the expenses of your spouse in attending meetings of professional groups be reimbursed? And, as mentioned previously, the firm's obligations to cover you under medical and disability insurance programs and for malpractice insurance should be expressly stated. The agreement should be explicit as to who must pay the premium for this coverage.

Even if some of these payments, standing alone, might *seem* to make you an employee for tax purposes, if you and the firm intend, and clearly express your intention in a written agreement, that you are an independent contractor, the firm's agreement to reimburse expenses and to cover you under various benefit programs would not affect your expressed status.

Compensation

So far we have discussed the items that should be covered in the of counsel agreement respecting duties: your duties to the firm and its duties toward you. Now comes the question of compensation. Whatever the arrangement you have with the firm regarding compensation, it should be spelled out in writing in the of counsel agreement. There are, perhaps, as many variations of compensation arrangements as there are lawyers.

Often a lawyer will become of counsel to the firm from which he or she retires as a partner. In that case, the partnership agreement may spell out what the retired lawyer is to receive. If the partnership agreement is silent, then the of counsel agreement must supply the omission.

Assuming that, as of counsel, you will have duties, then it is reasonable to presume that the firm expects to pay you for performance. Where the duties are those for which the firm will be compensated—such as working on a client's matters—then the agreement may provide that you will receive some percentage of the fee. If this is the case, the of counsel agreement should give you the right to approve the hourly rate being charged for your services. If you are producing the business but not working on the matters produced, the of counsel agreement should be certain to give you other duties giving rise to your right of compensation. Otherwise, you might find yourself in the position of engaging in prohibited fee splitting with your firm, especially if you are an independent contractor. Where the duties are noncompensated, such as client development activities, then it may be appropriate to pay you an agreed annual stipend, payable monthly or at some other interval. In the most preferable arrangement and the one likely to give rise to the least controversy, the firm will elect to pay you a negotiated amount on an annual basis to cover all of your work for the firm and will not make any charge for firm services provided to you.

Hours of Work Annually

When a lawyer joins a law firm as of counsel, particularly coming from corporate, government, or academic life, it is important to understand the work ethic expected by the firm. Since of counsel is supposed to be retired and "taking it easy," he or she (theoretically, at least) will not be working as hard as other lawyers in the office. But both the lawyer and the firm should be clear on this. Therefore, the of counsel agreement should state specifically how many hours the firm expects you, as of counsel, to work per year. It should be clear that those hours may include time spent in performing services of benefit to the firm that do not necessarily result directly in compensation to the firm, such as attendance at professional meetings, legal writing, client development efforts, and the like. The number of hours required should bear some reasonable relationship to the rate of compensation, taking into account the value of the benefits being provided by the firm, in order to avoid dissatisfaction on both sides with the arrangement.

Conflicts of Interest

In deciding upon an of counsel arrangement, a lawyer must give careful consideration to any possible conflicts of interest that may arise. If the difficulties should appear insurmountable, perhaps it will be necessary to seek an arrangement elsewhere. One should confront the conflicts issue early on, and make sure there is no problem, in order to avoid frustration and disappointment further down the road.

Most conflict problems are caused by the attorney's simultaneous or successive representation of clients with adverse interests. But conflicts situations arise in other contexts. Suppose the lawyer wishes to serve as of counsel to two or more firms, as is permissible in New York. For purposes of applying the rules governing conflicts, it is as if all of these firms were a single firm. Even if lawyers associate together for office space but practice independently, if they have access to one another's files, they are treated as partners for conflicts purposes.

It is pretty clear to most lawyers that simultaneous representation of two clients with adverse interests is prohibited. Constant monitoring of any potential situation is essential to assure that no conflict exists that requires attention.

In the matter of successive representation of clients with adverse interests, a different sort of problem is presented. Here it is a matter of preserving loyalty to the former client and confidentiality of matters disclosed during the representation. These factors must be evaluated carefully.

Presumptions

When lawyers are associated, there is an irrebuttable presumption in the case of present associates that confidences have been shared. Thus, the client of any one lawyer is the client of all for the purpose of determining conflicts. In the case of past associates, the current trend seems to declare that the presumption of shared confidences is rebuttable. It then becomes a matter of fact as to what the lawyer, now seeking to be of counsel, knew as to matters handled by other lawyers in his former firm.*

*There are a number of cases mentioned in Harold G. Wren and Beverly J. Glascock's book (*The Of Counsel Agreement*, Chapter 10, pages 70–71) dealing with this problem. We commend them to your attention, if you are ever confronted with these questions. The book is available from the Senior Lawyers Division of the American Bar Association.

Chinese Walls

The rules applied to former government lawyers are, in a sense, less restrictive. The Chinese Wall, which does not receive many accolades when lawyers in the private sector are involved, appears to be more tolerable where government attorneys are concerned. The Chinese Wall refers to various internal protections adopted by firms to ensure that a lawyer with privileged information from one client is shielded from lawyers in the office who represent other clients, when such representation would create conflicts.

Many lawyers moving from the corporate world or from government to the private sector often are called as witnesses with respect to matters formerly handled by them in their corporate and government jobs. Most states prohibit a lawyer—and the law firm with which he is associated—from handling a matter as counsel when the lawyer is to be a witness for the client. One should keep this in mind in considering where to establish an of counsel arrangement.

Potential Client Conflicts

Finally, attention is required to a 1991 opinion of the Committee on Professional and Judicial Ethics of the Association of the Bar of the City of New York, Formal Opinion 1991-1, dated April 30, 1991, and reported in the October 1991 issue of *The Record* of the Association. This opinion, stated as simply as possible, says that if you are representing a particular client, and you are seeking to represent another client whose interests are, or may be, adverse to the present client, this fact must be disclosed to both, who must consent, or the future employment must be declined.

Since lawyers becoming of counsel in many instances are attempting to market their services to new clients, it is important, in the light of this opinion, to make sure that the effort to obtain representation of the new clients will not have to be disclosed to present clients of the firm.

Term

As with any agreement, the of counsel agreement should have a definite term; but this one is a little different. All does not come to an end with a termination in this situation. Some aspects of the relationship undoubtedly will be retained. For example, the of counsel may continue to have an office and some office services available to him or her. Similarly, the of counsel may have some responsibility after termination of the formal arrangement. Whatever the understanding, it should be spelled out.

The term of the agreement will have an obvious effect on malpractice insurance coverage. Therefore, when drafting the provisions of the agreement respecting its termination, simultaneous attention should be given to the provisions relative to malpractice coverage commencement and conclusion. Should it not be feasible to determine now what all the details of the arrangement are to be after the term ends, the agreement should nonetheless address the issue of malpractice coverage while otherwise providing for orderly conclusion of the arrangement. As lawyers, we know that the parties can always reach a new agreement and it is unnecessary to so state in the current agreement. Once all details have been worked out, the parties may choose to work under an "evergreen" arrangement that will continue until one or the other, upon an agreed notice, determines to end it.

These are the principal points to be covered in an of counsel agreement. If anything else is of particular importance to you, handle yourself as you would handle a good client. Make sure the agreement covers it.

7

Moving into Private Practice from Other Fields

Many lawyers, as they approach retirement from various fields of endeavor, begin to think about entering private practice. It may be that they practiced with a law firm only briefly, upon graduation from law school, or not at all. It may be a missed opportunity they wish to experience, or a first love to be recaptured.

Yet many are understandably apprehensive over such a step. But is a law career in corporate America, the judiciary, government service, or academia so different that these professionals can never succeed in private practice?

It is a mistake to harbor misgivings without carefully considering the similarities and differences between private practice and law practice in these other areas. Only after such consideration can you decide whether you can adapt—to the extent adaptation is needed.

Many highly successful people have made such changes in their professional lives more than once and are happy and satisfied with their choices. Although a complete shifting of one's gears may not be for the faint of heart, neither should it be reserved only for the most intrepid. As the old saying goes, it is dangerous just to get up in the morning, so at times we must just gather our self-confidence and move forward.

Although it may be more common to think of men when we consider members of the bar who are able to embark upon second careers, many women do so as well. Despite the dual burden of sustaining a career and managing a family, women are able to shift gears when the occasion demands. The sidebars present two examples of women in the legal profession—Charlotte P. Armstrong and Jean Allard—who have made such transitions.

Charlotte P. Armstrong

Charlotte P. Armstrong was in the first class to graduate women from Harvard Law School. After her graduation in 1953, she joined an estate planning practitioner in Boston; and the following year she was a member of the campaign staff that helped get Clifford P. Case, of New Jersey, elected to the United States Senate. That accomplished, Ms. Armstrong moved on to the Justice Department in Washington and thence to the Internal Revenue Service in New York. In 1967, she became an Assistant Counsel and Assistant Vice President at Bankers Trust Company; and three years later, she became an Associate Corporate Secretary and Associate Counsel at General Dynamics Corporation. When General Dynamics moved from New York to St. Louis, Ms. Armstrong joined Cravath, Swaine & Moore. In all this time, she was becoming an authority on various forms of employee compensation and benefit plans. She continued in this area, and in 1976 became an Assistant General Counsel and Assistant Vice President with The Equitable Life Assurance Society; then in 1978 she joined the Human Resources Consulting Group at Peat, Marwick, Mitchell & Co. In 1986 she returned to private practice, and since 1988 has served as a consultant to Hirschfeld, Sterm, Moyer & Ross, Inc.

Notwithstanding her career changes, Ms. Armstrong has found time to devote herself to work with a number of educational, artistic, and philanthropic organizations serving the public interest, such as the Community Service Society of New York; the Winsor School; and, of course, Harvard Law School, serving as president of the alumni association.

Jean Allard

Having made her latest career change at age 66, Jean Allard, a former Chair of the ABA's Business Law Section, is pursuing a new challenge as President of the Metropolitan Planning Council in Chicago, which deals with public policy issues and regional problems in northeastern Illinois.

Ms. Allard graduated from the University of Chicago Law School in 1953. Initially, she worked for the law school in research and administration and then moved on to private law practice. In 1962, Ms. Allard became Secretary and General Counsel of Maremont Corporation; and ten years later she rejoined the University of Chicago as Vice President for Business and Finance. Three years thereafter she became a partner of Sonnenschein, Nath & Rosenthal in Chicago; and in 1990, she embarked on her current assignment.

She asserts that some career changes were presented to her in the form of job offers; others, which she initiated, were the result of law firm interviews or pursuit by a search firm. She claims that she has enjoyed each change and each has had elements of excitement.

Anyone seeking a career change, she says, "must be willing to take risks and be involved in learning new ideas and new vocabularies. Then do it—and enjoy the challenges."

What are some of the similarities and differences between private law practice and other areas of legal endeavor?

When the Corporate Lawyer Moves

The Concept of Time

The economic concept that the most valuable asset of a lawyer is his or her time receives its most brilliant illustration in private law practice. Whether a lawyer merely hangs up a shingle in the old hometown or joins a substantial firm in a major city, he or she will find it necessary to keep careful account of how time is spent. More importantly, in every instance that lawyer will compare the benefit of what is to be accomplished in any time interval with the cost (rate multiplied by time) to get it done. It then becomes apparent that the time allotted to work on a particular aspect of a problem must be fitted to its economic worth, i.e., what a client will be willing to pay for it. Most lawyers readily understand the concept and have no difficulty circumscribing their work to match the revenue it will produce. Others find such mundane effort repugnant.

In a corporate law department, attorneys are seldom asked to do this. In general, one uses as much time as necessary—within reason—to solve a particular problem without regard for hours or minutes and dollars or cents. Also in the corporate law department (although there are exceptions), one generally is not required to complete daily time sheets, with every telephone call recorded, every drafting effort mentioned. Such luxury in practice cannot be indulged in the private law office. Anyone planning the shift must accept that.

An exception may be found in the case of the corporate lawyer who is continually harassed by impatient corporate officers insisting on immediate answers. This experience is common for general counsel. To them, it is a luxury to serve as of counsel in a private law firm when there is ample time to analyze and attempt to solve a problem.

No Longer Holding Hands

The very nature of their position means that in-house lawyers are treated differently from outside lawyers. The in-house lawyer is often a "hand-holder"—closely associated with an executive of the business, whether it be a division manager or a department head. This relationship has advantages. The lawyer learns in detail how a project or situation operates, how it relates to the overall functioning of the corporation, what the nature of the problem is, and how he or she is expected to assist in solving that problem. After reviewing events, the lawyer will respond with advice, and, even more significant, he or she will usually know what happened as a result. And if the "client" fails to tell the corporate lawyer how things turned out, the lawyer need only walk down the hall to the client's office and ask.

The lawyer in private practice does not receive the same feedback from the client. When this information isn't provided, the lawyer may hesitate to pick up the telephone and make an inquiry. After all, the client might think that the lawyer was drumming up more business, or in any event might be charged for the lawyer's time even though the client didn't initiate the call.

Distancing Yourself from the Business

As a corporate lawyer, you may learn precisely how your company makes a widget, and you may be familiar with the chemical formula, the manufacturing techniques, the distribution methods, the accounting rules, and so on. You have the opportunity to visit the plant where the widget is made and to meet with the people who produce it, ship it, and sell it; their problems are, truly, your problems. If you now shift to your company's outside law firm, life will be quite different. Seldom will you make trips to the plant; and detailed descriptions of manufacturing methods and techniques will be provided only when absolutely necessary for your work on a case. Somehow, problems are more abstract, less people-oriented. You may be more a lawyer, but less an amateur psychologist or sociologist.

Organizational Strictures

The size and organizational characteristics of the corporate law department from which one may be departing, and the size of the law firm to which one may be going, are also significant factors to take into account. Many large law departments today are organized along lines of legal disciplines: corporate law, securities, antitrust, environmental, and so forth. Almost all law firms of any size are similarly organized. If you have been practicing with a large corporate law department as a specialist, say, in antitrust litigation, you will not have any difficulty in shifting into life as an antitrust litigator with a major law firm. However, many in-house counsel are the last of the true generalists—handling questions of corporate, securities, environmental, and employment law with equal aplomb. If this has been your duty, and if you then find yourself confined to the rigid departmental lines of a large law firm, you may well become frustrated. You might be well advised to seek shelter in a smaller law office, where there is less specialization.

But even if you are somewhat a specialist, there is nonetheless a challenge in moving from the corporate arena to private practice. In most corporations, you need deal only with a limited number of industries or industry groups: food and beverages; metal mining and manufacturing; securities and financial services. You need only learn in depth the law relating to these industries. Once you cross the line into private practice, your world is not so circumscribed. You will find yourself attending seminars on a variety of subjects on which you must be informed to be able to advise the multiplicity of client types that you must deal with.

This is not to frighten you, but merely to point out that your education may have to continue apace following a shift into private practice.

Bossing Yourself

Perhaps, after many years in a corporate law department, you are beginning to tire of the rigid lines of authority that seem de rigueur in business corporations. You might have reported to a divisional manager, or perhaps you were a general counsel or an associate general counsel, reporting directly to a chief executive officer. In any event, you knew exactly who reported to whom. Join a large law firm, and all that is gone. For the most part, you are your own supervisor. The lines of authority in most major law firms are loose indeed. There will probably be a chair of a practice group, say, in securities law, with which you will be associated; but the chair's function is to find, among the lawyers assigned to the practice group, the right combination of attorneys to undertake a project, e.g., preparation of a securities registration statement. There will be different combinations of attorneys, organized into different committees, to handle matters related to hiring of partners and associates, compensation, firm administration, office rental and outfitting, social events, and so forth. Seldom are all of these functions centered in a single group of partners or principals. You can usually like or hate your single boss in the corporation; in the law firm, you have a multitude of possibilities on both counts.

Corporate counsel shifting to private practice—especially those moving to a large law firm—will be surprised at the amount of time spent in associate evaluation. As one former general counsel put it, "I had always felt that we were fairly strict in our annual personnel evaluations in the law department, but the partners' evaluations of associates were rough and tough. Even the comments for the few associates who everyone agreed were performing well were tempered in order that no associate might assume that he or she was clearly on a partnership track."

Simplified Life-Style

The move from a corporation to a law firm can also offer a change in life-style. Whether it is a tolerable change may depend upon you, since each individual will react differently. In the corporation, a lawyer, and particularly a lawyer of senior status, will enjoy a number of "perks": the company car, use of the executive jet or first-class air travel, gourmet meals in the executive dining room, and the like. Moving from a corporation to an outside law firm, you may experience culture shock: gone is the company car, use of the jet or first-class travel depends on the policies of one's client, and gourmet meals are paid out of your own pocket in after-tax dollars. However, the comforting thought is that, absent all that travel and rich food and drink, you will be healthier and, hopefully, happier.

When the Judge Moves

Alms-giver to Alms-seeker

The lawyer who has been on the bench for a considerable period of time must prepare himself or herself for an adjustment in role and attitude in returning to private law practice. Once the dispenser of justice, you are now the petitioner for justice; once in control of activities in your courtroom, you must (assuming that you become a litigator) place yourself under the direction of another person sitting where you once "reigned."

Jack Donald Voss

Some lawyers have used their particular experience before retirement to establish a new career after retirement. Jack Donald Voss, of Lancaster, Ohio, is one person who has done so. Mr. Voss had a multifaceted career following graduation from Harvard Law School in 1948. He practiced as an associate with, and later was a partner of, Sidley & Austin in Chicago from 1949 to 1962. He then became general counsel of Anchor Hocking Corporation in Lancaster, Ohio. Rising through the management ranks, he became president of Anchor Hocking International in 1972 and served in this position until retiring in 1988. His experience in the international arena enabled him, following his retirement from Anchor Hocking, to establish a consulting business, Voss International. His new venture specializes in licensing, joint ventures, mergers, and acquisitions. Mr. Voss is enthusiastic about prospects for second careers for lawyers, and he has served as Co-Vice Chair of the Committee on Second Careers of the ABA's Senior Lawyers Division.

In short, on another's head lies your crown. Not everyone can adapt easily to that shift in position.

As a judge, you read the pleadings and the briefs, and listen to witnesses and counsel. Then you make up your mind and issue your decision. When you return to private law practice, you may read the same pleadings, the same briefs, hear the same witnesses and opposing counsel. But regardless of how you make up your own mind, you still have a duty to present the best case you can for your client. You must be an advocate, whatever your judgment.

As a judge, you were probably blessed with the services of a first-rate mind in the person of a law clerk. He or she was no doubt the graduate of a prestigious law school, was capable of getting to the core of a problem quickly, could accurately review the cases presented to you in briefs of counsel, was able to research and find the authorities on which you might rely, and

James F. Stapleton

Flexibility was a key factor in the career changes achieved by James F. Stapleton. First a litigator for a year in 1958 in the Department of Justice, he became a practitioner-partner in the 1958–1973 period in a Bridgeport, Connecticut, law firm, combining community service as corporation counsel for the City of Bridgeport, member of the City's Board of Education, and three years as Republican Town Chairman. He was appointed to the Connecticut Superior Court, and finally he returned to private law practice as a partner in one of Connecticut's most prestigious law firms.

Community service and its political overtones facilitated the appointment of Judge Stapleton to the bench. It was not the goal that he had in mind when he became active in politics, but when the judicial appointment was offered, it was an opportunity to be seized.

Judge Stapleton describes the bench as offering a challenging and interesting job of importance to the community. But he faced another career change when he decided to leave the judiciary. This, he reports, was motivated by a variety of circumstances in his personal life. He had five teenage children getting ready to start college; he also faced a family tragedy in the form of a child's serious illness—which culminated in the loss of a young son shortly after the Judge's next career change. Judge Stapleton was also "unhappy with the merger of all the trial courts in Connecticut, which had the effect of reducing the compensation and prestige" of the judges of the Superior Court, the highest court of general jurisdiction in Connecticut. He decided it was time to return to private law practice.

Day, Berry & Howard—one of the largest law firms in Connecticut, based in Hartford—had announced plans to open an office in Stamford. Judge Stapleton put in a call to Ralph Dixon, who was at that time Day, Berry's senior trial partner. Soon there was an agreement, and in 1978, at the age of forty-five, Judge Stapleton became the first lateral partner ever admitted to the firm. Says Attorney Stapleton, "It has been a mutually enjoyable and profitable association since that time."

served as a sounding board as you approached a decision. In the private law firm, you may or may not find the young lawyer you are seeking to be that valuable assistant. Some firms are able to hire and retain superb talent; others cannot. But whether you have or lack the legal assistance you need, the quality of your work must be maintained. Thus, you may find yourself doing some of the nitty-gritty examination of the law yourself in order to be confident of your advice to your clients.

Benefits Lost

Many lawyers deplore the fact that the judiciary is not compensated adequately. There is the temptation to return to private law practice for economic reasons. However, one should not jump to conclusions. At a point in life when one's family has been educated and the need for income has been reduced, the advantages stemming from the generous pension benefits available to retired members of the judiciary in many states may outweigh other economic considerations. The lawyer in private practice must set aside substantial sums—much in after-tax dollars—in order to provide the principal capable of generating an equivalent to the state or federal pension. Similarly, medical insurance benefits provided to judges as state employees are often free of cost to the judge, while similar benefits obtained through law firms are at the expense of the individual attorney, again in after-tax dollars.

Other compensation issues are discussed later in this chapter.

Leaving Your Pedestal

From Ruler to the Ruled

Perhaps the biggest adjustment a lawyer must make when moving from government service to private practice is in accepting the abrupt change in the scope and significance of his or her work. In most situations, the government lawyer, particularly at the higher levels of either federal or state service, will have engagements of considerable scope. His or her efforts will significantly affect many citizens. In private law practice, that is seldom the case.

Another area of adjustment concerns the decision process. Because of the broad scope of the work, the government lawyer's choices of courses of action are important in their impact on other people. The higher the rank of the official, the greater the impact in the usual situation. Most practicing lawyers in the private sector, however, do not have the opportunity to make decisions that affect anyone other than their own clients.

And closely related to these two factors of scope of work and decision making is the issue of prestige and power. Government service at any level, but most certainly at the higher echelons of government, brings with it a large measure of distinction and authority. Seldom does the lawyer in private practice enjoy the same level of influence.

Finally, the benefits provided to a lawyer in government service are generally considerably greater, both in the absolute and in economic value, than benefits provided to a lawyer in private practice. In short, the lawyer in private practice must provide whatever benefits he needs, by purchasing them for himself with after-tax dollars. The lawyer in government often finds more liberal vacation plans available to him than to his counterpart in private practice. Moreover, the lawyer in private practice can generate no fees when on vacation, but the earnings of the lawyer in government continue even when he is on vacation. Government, both federal and state, generally provides more liberal pension benefits than one can obtain under self-funded Keogh plans or other personal pension plans common to lawyers in private practice.

To many lawyers, hours of work are important. Questions related to one's ability to spend time with family or pursuing other personal interests are serious issues. In government, the ability one has to regulate one's own schedule is dependent in great measure upon one's rank. The higher the rank, the more freedom one has, but, conversely, the greater the demands of the job. The lawyer in private practice usually has unlimited freedom to choose when and how long to work—how many hours per year to attend to the job is his or her choice. But that choice directly affects earnings and the image presented to other lawyers in the firm.

Edward R. Finch, Jr.

Edward R. Finch, Jr., is a lawyer who has had a variety of experiences in the law and has successfully moved from military life as a colonel in the Air Force, with duty overseas during World War II and at home later, to the law. He practiced with the firm of which he was a founding partner, Finch & Schaefler, and with its successor, LeBoeuf, Lamb, Leiby & MacRae, for more than thirty-five years. While active in the legal profession, Ed Finch found time to serve his country in various diplomatic assignments as a delegate from the United States to United Nations conferences in Switzerland, Japan, and Austria; and as a special ambassador to Panama. He then moved into the business arena, and for several years served as a director and as the vice president, secretary, and general counsel of American International Petroleum Corporation. In 1992, he resumed private practice. Meanwhile, since his area of the law is trusts and estates, as a hobby he has become an expert on the law of outer space, and has also written four books.

Ambassador Finch has these words of advice to persons aspiring to continue to practice after "retirement": "Exercise regularly and always maintain your private practice and connections, no matter where your professional life may lead you. Always look forward and work forward. Don't dwell on the past. The future is always quickly upon us."

WHEN THE ACADEMICIAN MOVES

From Professor to Practitioner

Perhaps the greatest difference experienced by the lawyer who leaves the world of teaching for the world of private practice is in the assembly of people dealt with every day. The outlook of the student, concentrating on issues in a particular field of law, debating what might have been the outcome in a particular case, given a few fact changes, is not the same as a client with a problem truly affecting the client's life. Gone from the lawyer- academician's life are the examination books and term papers. Instead, there comes across the lawyer-practitioner's desk a stream of correspondence and memoranda describing difficulties and proposing solutions. From these differences, one can surmise another: the freedom in academia to research questions just because they are interesting and challenging and the inability to do that in private practice because clients will not usually pay the tab unless it produces a practical result.

University professors—including those teaching in law school—face the burdens and the nuisances of administration. Ask any faculty member, and there are the same complaints about too many committee meetings and too many administrative assignments foisted upon academics, leaving less time than they wish to have for purely pedagogical duties. In this regard, the lawyer who leaves life on a campus for the world of the law firm or the corporate law department may find that more time is spent on administration and less on practicing law than he or she would like.

In many other areas, however, there is little difference between membership on a law school faculty and service with a law firm. Neither entity is bereft of politics. Benefits to the individual, such as life and medical insurance, in each are often the same, but sometimes different; it depends upon the law school and upon the law firm. Generally speaking, one should recognize that average partner income in a law firm will exceed the average salary of a professor of law.

Perquisites will vary, with law school usually offering the opportunity for longer vacations, less demands on one's time, and occasional travel on client matters. The title of professor of law, nevertheless, carries with it an element of prestige seldom associated with a law firm partnership.

When Should You Make the Move?

Be Certain You Have Clients

If a person is contemplating a move to private practice, the timing is important. Many lawyers, although having a choice, delay the decision until after age sixty-five. That, I think, is a mistake. Having made a decision to enter private practice, it is far better to make the change earlier rather than later, for a variety of reasons.

Harold G. Wren

Early in life, Harold G. Wren, who was Chair of the Senior Lawyers Division in the 1992–93 year, shifted from private practitioner to academician; he has, once more, returned to the realm of the private practitioner. But let us have Professor Wren tell his story in his own words.

"All of us have wondered from time to time how much our careers are determined by destiny and how much by our own choices. In my own case, after a relatively short period of practicing tax law with a Wall Street law firm, I chose to enter the academic world. During the next forty-two years, I was variously a law professor at four law schools and a law dean at three others. I have also been a labor arbitrator since 1958. And until I retired as a Captain in 1980, I was active in Naval Reserve Intelligence. Throughout these years, I thoroughly enjoyed all of the various roles that I chose to play or into which, for one reason or another, fate seemed to lead me. I certainly did not look forward to retirement in 1991.

"Faced with the difficulty of finding a new career, I decided to return to the practice of law. Because of my labor arbitration experience, some occasional consulting work for other attorneys, my activities with the organized bar, and my writing with respect to the profession, I had retained some knowledge of law practice as an outside observer. But it has only been since the beginning of my second career, *as a practicing attorney*, that I have felt that I am, at long last, truly a member of the bar.

"Like a kid with a new toy, I find that every case in which I am involved is fascinating, and I can hardly wait to get behind the old word processor when I go to work in the morning. Some of my nonlawyer friends feel that one should devote his or her retirement to golf, fishing, or playing bridge. I find that none of these activities is as thrilling as writing a brief, preparing a pleading, drafting a will, or performing any one of many tasks that my peers were doing during those forty-two years that I was in the classroom or performing administrative duties in legal education. I still miss the classroom, and I will gladly return to that part of the academic world if I should ever be invited. In the meantime, I cannot imagine anything would give me as much joy as what I am now doing, serving as of counsel to a small law firm."

First, if one shifts from any of the worlds we have been discussing to private practice, there is the problem of obtaining a client base. It is not particularly interesting to have a law office unless you have clients to serve. Clients don't appear magically just because you hang up a shingle, unless, in those rare cases, you happen to be a person of renowned ability who has people flocking to the door. At age fifty-five or sixty, you still have friends and acquaintances in business, college and law school fellow alumni and alumnae, and former associates who are still young enough to be active—often at the peak of their own careers. These are the people who control the substantial legal business of the country. These are the people who will provide the cases and problems fueling your business. On the other hand, if you wait until you have passed age sixty-five and have retired from a corporation, the bench, government, or an academic position, your contemporaries will have retired also. Your business will then have to come from people younger than yourself. These persons have their own sets of contemporaries to whom they may prefer to send their legal business.

Many law firms will not accept "lateral hires" unless assured of a portfolio of new business from the new partner or counsel. If the candidate does not have the business in hand, he or she must have reasonable prospects for new business development. By moving into private practice at age fifty-five or sixty, you improve your bargaining position with the vast majority of law firms. In that age bracket, you can assure a law firm that, assuming reasonably good health, you can offer ten to fifteen years of productive legal work, to the mutual benefit of you both. You also offer sound expectations that business will come your way. Should you wait until age sixty-five or seventy to make the switch to private practice, you cannot look forward with the same degree of optimism.

One word of caution: Consider the effects a shift at age fifty-five or sixty into private practice will have upon pension benefits you expect to receive from your earlier employment. Even if you are vested in your pension plan, the annual benefit is bound to be lower. Consequently, you will have to make up the difference in retirement income from savings achieved during law practice. That, of course, is going to depend upon your total income and how much you are able to save. This is the gamble, the risk that you take, if you want to become a private practitioner.

The scenario set out above—moving to a law firm at age fifty-five or sixty—suggests an earlier start than you might initially contemplate. But it has its advantages. It allows you to plan a wide distribution of announcements, get them drafted, perhaps write some individual notes to those on the list, and have them in the mail in timely fashion as you start your second career.

A word about those individual notes: Many potential clients are busy people who receive tons of announcements every month, most of which wind up being tossed away by their secretaries. To avoid that happening to your announcement, you must make sure it draws attention to yourself on an individual basis. Along with the formal message that you have joined this-or-that law firm, include a few handwritten words to the addressee—a message to connect you both—about your alma mater, a social event you both attended, or a word about family. This assures that your mailing will *not* immediately be discarded into the circular file.

What Sort of Compensation Can You Expect?

There are doubtless as many formulas for compensating individuals moving into private practice from other fields as there are such individuals. There is no established formula that everyone uses. Rather, it depends upon the prestige, talent, energy level, and "rainmaking" ability of the lawyer making the move.

In recent years, some major firms have taken on partners based on the lawyers' prestige in some particular walk of life, but without regard to whether these persons had sufficient, if not superior, legal ability. These firms have regretted these choices but learned from the experience. A lawyer who enjoys reknown but feels uneasy in undertaking a law practice probably should forgo the opportunity. Without sterling performance as a lawyer, he or she cannot expect to be well received among private firms. Prestige and talent must work together.

Similarly, it is important that a lawyer desiring to enter private practice, as a partner, is willing to work very hard. Few firms are willing to pay large compensation to enable a lawyer to devote vast amounts of time to improving a golf score, even though the lawyer may spend hours entertaining potential clients at the nineteenth hole. In most law firms today, partners—even senior lawyers—are expected to put in 1,800 or more hours a year, and it is hoped that most of these will be billable hours.

Of course, arrangements can be made between lawyers and firms that permit less input of time by the lawyer—and lesser compensation. These arrangements can be reflected in an of counsel agreement, or similar written understanding, as discussed briefly below and in more detail in Chapter 6.

The lateral hire of a partner or counsel to a law firm, regardless of what is said, remains an economic decision by the firm. Almost without exception, any firm taking on a senior lawyer expects that he or she will generate sufficient business to make the arrangement worthwhile for the law firm. The attorney who can leave a different area of practice and move to a law firm with a guaranteed stable of clients is quite rare. Usually, friends and associates do not commit themselves to specific amounts of legal business in advance; very often, they just don't know how much lawyering they are going to require. Consequently, in many situations, the agreement between the lawyer and the law firm contemplates that the arrangement will be on a trial basis for a period of time, measured in either months or years. That gives the lawyer coming to the firm from another area of practice the time to attract his or her own clients and new business for the firm. Once the lawyer's ability as a rainmaker has been measured, the arrangement and compensation basis can be made permanent.

Finding an Opportunity

Where does one turn to find an opportunity to join a firm as a new partner, or under some form of an of counsel arrangement? As with most business arrangements, the first sources are people you know, and most importantly, people who know you. These are the partners in the law firms that you have dealt with over your years of practice. There are the general counsel you have known in corporations around the country, who may know which of the firms that have represented the corporation are in the habit of bringing in counsel to their firms.

In considering what law firms to approach, compare your own special qualifications and areas of expertise with the fields of practice in which each of the firms is competent. For instance, it may be useless to pursue a firm that already is very strong in environmental law, if that is your specialty, but very productive for you if a firm is deficient in environmental lawyers.

It may also be useful to discuss your desires with officers of your local bar, who may be aware of firms seeking to strengthen their forces. Talk with personnel recruitment organizations specializing in legal searches; it may be that a law firm in your community needs a person with your qualifications.

Fellow law school alumni and alumnae are additional sources of help. Be sure to let them know that you want to widen your horizons, and don't hesitate to ask them for their assistance.

Documenting the Arrangement with an Agreement

Whatever the arrangement between law firm and lawyer, it should be documented in some form of writing.

When a lawyer retires from a firm in which he or she has been a partner, and continues in an of counsel relationship, the firm agreement among its partners may spell out some of the details of the post-retirement situation. If it is not complete, then some further documentation is necessary to cover the missing matters.

However, in the circumstances we have been discussing in this chapter, there is no pre-existing agreement between the lawyer and the law firm. Under these conditions—that is, when a lawyer joins a firm with which he or she has had no prior connection—a more detailed agreement is both necessary and desirable. Suggestions for the details of such an agreement were set forth in Chapter 6.

8

Moving from Private Practice to New Fields

Senior lawyers, whether ready to retire or several years away from the fateful day, often feel the desire for change. Scintillating though the law may be, you may grow tired of its charms and consider pursuing a different type of career.

THE POSSIBILITIES OF POLITICS

Politics Carries a Financial Cost

Few will deny that, in the United States today, a person cannot run for public office—even on the local level—without incurring considerable expense. Moreover, that expense escalates with the degree of responsibility of the elective office. It takes some coin of the realm to run for the town council, but considerably more to run for the state legislature—and a very large sum to run for the United States Congress.

Consequently, a candidate must either have substantial resources or the ability to raise funds. The person approaching or in retirement is not always fortunate enough to be able to generate the funds required for a successful campaign.

Even if you are willing to raise or provide the funds, the task of securing a nomination or party endorsement is daunting. The opportunity to be a candidate often goes to the youthful politician who has paid his or her dues by working diligently in election after election. The person who jumps into the political sea as a senior is relatively rare.

Most lawyers who elect to pursue politics do not find several other requirements a problem: One must be able to speak effectively in public (most attorneys are accustomed to talking on their feet) and to meet others with grace and ease (which seldom bothers the practicing lawyer). With few exceptions, lawyers commonly deal with new and different areas of knowledge and are accustomed to mastering new subjects in the course of practice. This ability serves well in the political arena, since the enactment of new legislation today and the execution of laws cover a wide spectrum of human activity.

Lawyers deal frequently with settlements of issues, and the politician must learn to compromise with those of opposing viewpoints; thus, the lawyer's skills in settling cases will be an advantage in the realm of politics.

Not so inviting to the lawyer will be the requirement, in the usual situation, of considerable travel. Many lawyers in private practice have little necessity for business travel; they are unaccustomed to spending extended periods away from home. A jump into the political arena will usually compel forays among the electorate at vote-gathering time and attendance at a seat of government that may be miles away from home. Also, many evenings and weekends must be spent away from home, attending public functions, including weddings, funerals, and the like.

All of these facts need to be taken into account by a lawyer contemplating a political career. But if you make the choice and achieve your goal of a political victory, the rewards may, indeed, be great. There comes with political success a feeling of personal accomplishment, the satisfaction of having made a contribution to one's country and of being accepted by one's peers, and the knowledge that one is known for his or her achievements by a significant number of fellow citizens.

Possibilities in Government Service

Senior lawyers have a variety of reasons for deciding that a period of government service would indeed be a worthwhile supplement to a lifetime at the bar. In government, the opportunities are many.

Thomas J. Meskill

An active, practical interest in government and politics was the key to the ability of Thomas J. Meskill, now a Judge on the U.S. Court of Appeals for the Second Circuit, to change his career several times.

Judge Meskill worked on the mayoral campaign in his home town of New Britain, Connecticut, during his last year in law school and became involved in the Republican Town Committee immediately after graduation. He started out in the law as a sole practitioner, and when asked to run for the state senate in what everyone considered a hopeless campaign, he agreed to serve as the candidate. This gained him experience and name recognition—both useful to any fledgling lawyer.

Public service continued to beckon, and after several stints in the Corporation Counsel's office in New Britain, Attorney Meskill was elected Mayor Meskill in 1962. Defeated in a reelection bid, he turned his attention to Washington and served two terms as the elected Representative from the Sixth Congressional District of Connecticut.

Government remained a major interest, and in 1970 Tom Meskill was elected Governor of Connecticut. In 1974, he was nominated to fill a vacancy on the Second Circuit Court of Appeals, and returned to the law. He now serves as a senior judge of that court, having retired in 1993 as its Chief Judge.

Judge Meskill acknowledges that many people helped him as he pondered the career changes in his life. Reflecting on the factors that should influence such decisions, he suggests that we should keep our options open: "Don't be afraid to take reasonable risks if the career change offers potential rewards that you find missing in your life. Don't place too high a priority on financial rewards. Once you have made your decision to seek a career change, go all out—don't be halfhearted about it. Don't second-guess your decision, and never look back."

What About a Judgeship?

Here the obvious possibilities range from nomination for a seat on the federal bench to appointment or election to any one of a wide range of state, county, and local courts. When someone mentions nomination or election, our thoughts immediately—and correctly—turn to the political process. Many of the problems and rewards mentioned earlier apply equally here. But getting a seat on the bench requires an enormous outlay of effort. The dossier that must be assembled by the person seeking a federal judgeship is staggering, yet not necessarily effective in every case. On the state and local levels, the task differs in type, size, and complexity, depending on whether the seat is appointive or elective and on the differing requirements of state and local laws. While we might think that age and experience would run in favor of an aspirant, the costs related to mandatory retirement and pensions dictate that the citizenry look to younger people, able to provide lengthier tenure, when searching for candidates. One who has less than ten years to retirement age has an uphill battle in obtaining a seat on the bench.

This is not to say that there are not opportunities in the judiciary, short of a judgeship, and assuming one is willing to assist the court on an unpaid basis. In the federal system, each district has a number of senior lawyers who assist the sitting judges by reviewing case files, conferring with the parties, and endeavoring to work out mutually satisfactory settlements, which can then be translated into formal dispositions by the court. Attorneys performing this service are provided with office space in the federal courthouse and with other office services (perhaps including parking privileges). These positions are unpaid, except that in large and complicated cases the parties may agree that such an attorney be appointed a special master, with the compensation for the position, and the costs of an office outside the federal courthouse, to be shared by the parties to the litigation.

Many states have decided to use the services of senior lawyers working for the judiciary on a pro bono basis to review case files and work with the parties and the judges to reduce the case backlog. Some states, such as Florida, give reciprocal treatment to retired judges from other states and allow them to sit as trial referees. Lawyers who are not judges do not benefit from this policy, and Florida is one state where admission on motion, without taking the bar examination, is not possible. Consequently, a "mere lawyer" cannot be appointed a trial referee in Florida, unless already admitted to practice there.

A variation on service as a judge in a court of general jurisdiction is service as an administrative law judge. In the federal court system, experienced lawyers are being sought to become administrative law judges. Compensation is substantial, starting at $75,205 and rising to $104,130 after six years. Appointments are for life. Many of these judges handle disability claims for the Social Security Administration. Training for this aspect of the law has been conducted by the American Bar Association at its annual meetings and by its Senior Lawyers Division Committee on Social Security Law and Practice. Papers from these presentations will be very useful to judges in this area of the law. Information on where to apply for appointment as an administrative law judge is listed in the Appendix.

Government Service Outside the Judiciary

Both the U.S. Department of Commerce and the Department of State, working with the American Bar Association, are endeavoring to assemble groups of lawyers willing to travel abroad, on an expenses-only paid basis, to assist countries formerly in the Eastern Bloc in developing an entire legal framework based on democracy and capitalism. The unit working as a clearinghouse in this effort is the Central and East European Law Initiative, headquartered with the American Bar Association's office in Washington.

The Commerce Department, the State Department, and other branches of the federal government are willing to accept applications for employment from experienced lawyers for nonlegal positions in which legal experience may, nevertheless, be an appropriate background. For example, the State Department will consider lawyers seeking a second career in the foreign service. But anyone undertaking such a career path must be ready to undergo an exhaustive training in a foreign language and be prepared to accept assignment to an area of the world that may lack many of the comforts and amenities that we, today, take for granted.

Persons interested in working for the State Department, the U.S. Information Agency, or the foreign commerce service, which operates as a separate function of the State Department, can contact the Board of Examiners of State at the address given in the Appendix.

Isaac D. Russell

When Isaac D. ("Ike") Russell graduated from Yale University, he wasn't quite sure whether he wanted to join the foreign service or become an attorney. His entrance to Harvard Law School evidenced his decision. Ike joined a major Hartford law firm after graduation, became a partner, and later chaired the firm's Municipal Bond Department. Twenty-nine years later, in 1988, at age 54, he decided he'd had enough of the law and opted to take the foreign service examination. Supported by his wife and grown children, Isaac Russell passed the written and then the oral parts of the examination.

A popular member of his firm, Ike's decision to leave was met with surprise. He had taken a sabbatical leave some nine years before to work on small business development for a foundation in South Africa. This experience had two valuable consequences: It had proved that his lawyering skills were useful in other fields and other countries, and the firm learned that Ike had trained other lawyers in his department who could carry on the practice in his absence.

Isaac Russell's decision to leave the private sector for the lesser remuneration of government service was made easier by the fact that his children had been educated, by his spouse's support of his decision, and by the recognition that the foreign service was a profession equally as prestigious as the law. He embarked on an intensive course in the French language and the task of learning to "tell America's story" as an Information Officer or a Cultural Affairs Officer, whom Ike characterizes as a "superannuated junior officer."

Since joining the U.S. Information Agency, Mr. Russell has been posted to Harare, Zimbabwe, and to Abidjan, Ivory Coast; and in the summer of 1992, he joined the embassy staff in Addis Ababa, Ethiopia. He expects a new assignment in 1994.

Appraising his career in the foreign service to date, Ike Russell says that it has been "so far, so good. In fact, wonderful." Philosophically, he observes, "On the theory that life is very short, I suggest that you say yes to change if you get the chance."

The National Park Service seeks volunteers for help in maintaining the national parks and in serving as host or hostess at park campsites. One may apply to the National Park Service's volunteer coordinator and will be advised as to how to serve at the particular location of interest. While this is truly a pro bono assignment, the Park Service will arrange for accommodations at modest cost (or, sometimes, at no cost), and moderately priced meals are available at the parks.

Akin to work with the Park Service, but not with a government agency, is an undertaking with the Appalachian Mountain Club. It welcomes volunteers to assist in maintaining and improving various hiking trails on private lands and in the national parks and forests, including the famed Appalachian Trail.

Perhaps the greatest deterrent to a second career in government that the practicing lawyer faces is the regimentation and bureaucracy associated with working in either federal or state service. A lawyer in private practice, even in a very large firm, is essentially his or her own boss. The layers of authority in lower echelons of government and the cross-checking required at high levels of government can be annoying and frustrating. The stout of heart may be willing to take it all on with great equanimity. Other seniors may say, "Who needs it?"

Nonetheless, a second career in government has its rewards. Many lawyers who have spent years dealing with the fine details of business in corporate America, or with individuals with problems of relatively insignificant effect upon the world, may decide that it is time to do something that represents a service to the country. Work in government, which by definition serves the many, provides that opportunity. Secondly, lawyers, whether in law firms or in corporate law departments, may find themselves without particular and personal recognition. By embarking upon a second career in government, they assume a position of authority and therefore of importance: They are able to influence the larger picture.

Taking on the Robe of an Academician

Perhaps no change is greater for the practicing lawyer than the switch to the role of the teacher of law. The greatest culture shock

M. J. Schmidt

M. J. Schmidt is a Wisconsin lawyer who, since retirement, has devoted himself to government service, and who suggests that other retiring lawyers follow this course. Mr. Schmidt has done volunteer work with the U.S. Forest Service and the Park Service. In 1990 he constructed trails on the North Rim of the Grand Canyon and spent considerable time in the Canyon area with the Forest Service. Later that year, he worked on Mt. Shasta in a meadow restoration program. Although noting that he received no pay, he observed that his travel and related expenses were tax-deductible.

Mr. Schmidt's voluntary service to the government has not prevented him from pursuing other activities. Since he served with the U.S. Navy and the Coast Guard Reserve (he has more than twenty-four years of federal service) and is a member of the Maritime Law Association, Mr. Schmidt looks forward to serving as an arbitrator in maritime disputes.

Mr. Schmidt reminds us that through the Small Business Administration program called SCORE, retired business executives volunteer their services and expertise to small businesses requesting help. He suggests that other federal government departments, such as the Department of Justice, might use volunteer lawyers in times of overload; he proposes that these attorneys receive minimum remuneration and be required to waive any other entitlements.

to the practitioner who shifts to academia is the abrupt drop in the age of one's daily associates. It is a move from the adult world to the universe of youth. Some may find that stimulating and enjoyable, while others may only experience discomfort and annoyance.

The next challenge to be met is the necessity for preparation, a time-consuming process. Today's students, particularly in law, are energetic and bright. To teach them means staying ahead of them, a task demanding in itself. Moreover, the successful faculty member must devote himself or herself to extensive study and research. Many senior lawyers take pleasure in legal inquiry and do not mind reading extensively on legal subjects. For them, the switch from practice to academia will come easily.

Theory versus reality: For some, dealing with the hypothetical in the classroom will be exciting and stimulating; for others, only the reality of private practice can be satisfying. You should assess your feelings in this area and decide whether the classroom is a viable alternative.

Many people who move from the active practice of law back to the campus are surprised that they are unable to leave behind many of the problems of their old offices. Colleges and universities have their fair share of internal politics, committee assignments and meetings, and struggles over institutional policy. The lawyer who did not find these to be overwhelming outside the ivy-covered walls will not be bothered by them upon returning; but let there be no doubt, these obstacles to peaceful existence do exist, even in academia, and may even be worse there.

Also, finding a teaching position is not an easy task. First, one must recognize that university faculties are divided into tenure tracks and nontenure tracks. Only full-time faculty members can occupy tenure-track positions, and retired lawyers are not always ready to devote the time necessary to fulfill a full-time faculty post. On the other hand, accreditation requirements place a limit on the number of adjunct (i.e., part-time) professors that any law school may use. There is also the fact that junior lawyers who will have a longer period of service and development may be preferred over senior lawyers whose very ages place limits upon future service and whose services may be more expensive for the insitution. Recognize, too, that an adjunct professor's compensation for teaching a course is generally quite low; at many law schools, a fee of $2,000 to $2,500 per semester per course would be the rule, depending upon the school.

Despite the hurdles and fences one could erect in front of the doors to a new career in teaching, the mainstay of a choice to make this move is the opportunity to open new horizons for young people and to be able to have many aspiring students benefit from the experience of a real, practicing attorney who has had a lifetime at the law.

Donald E. Pease

In mid-1983, Donald E. Pease retired early from E. I. DuPont de Nemours, Inc., to do more pro bono work, to volunteer his services for an arbitration program adopted by the Delaware courts, and to "devote more time to my golf game. When I retired I had no intention to start a second career."

He was approached by the dean of the Widener University School of Law, who informed him that he needed someone to teach a course in corporate finance. The dean believed that Mr. Pease's experience at DuPont, which had largely been in corporation law, was a suitable background. As Mr. Pease tells the story, "When I asked him what casebook would be used, he removed from his bookcase a large text on the subject. I looked through it hastily and saw all sorts of strange graphs, tables on present value of a future dollar, and formulae on the usefulness of beta in valuation. I quickly told the dean that I didn't believe I was competent to teach the course.

"He said, 'Take the book home, page through it and see what is familiar to you, and come back tomorrow.' After this meeting I discussed with my wife whether I should take the job, if offered. Although she said that I should, one always suspects that the wife of a retired person wants to get her husband out of her daytime domain and routine." *(continued on next page)*

AN OPPORTUNITY TO CONTRIBUTE

In the chapter that follows, we will discuss the opportunity to serve the community as lawyers in a pro bono (i.e., without compensation) capacity. However, there are other opportunities for attorneys to provide assistance, often at minimal charge, which does not involve the rendering of advice but which is valuable to the beneficiaries.

We have already discussed the programs being developed by both federal and state courts to utilize the services of retired lawyers. As mentioned, while office services and certain other amenities are provided, there is seldom any compensation paid to those who assist the court, except in the case of retired judges serving as trial referees.

(continued from previous page)

Nonetheless, Mr. Pease did what the dean suggested, found some cases and other materials with which he was familiar, and agreed to try to teach the course for one semester.

After beginning his teaching activities in January of 1984, halfway through the semester Donald Pease was asked to teach full time. He accepted, and in 1993 was still teaching as a visiting professor.

States Professor Pease: "I have found from a career standpoint that nothing compares with the classroom experience. The rapport with the students in and out of the classroom is stimulating, and the association with the other professors is most worthwhile. At the same time, I note that teaching requires a good deal of work in preparing for classes, in working with the students in their various activities, and in writing articles for journals. The students quickly sort out those professors who are ill-prepared or don't contribute in other ways to their success or to the good reputation of the law school.

"But, if the teacher does his or her homework, presents the material of the courses in an interesting and organized manner, and in other ways shows genuine concern for the law school and its students, the rewards are great."

Arbitration, mediation, and alternative dispute resolution generally are burgeoning fields related to the law. The services of retired lawyers can be used in all of these areas. In some instances, those who volunteer their services receive no compensation in the initial stages of a case but are paid if the matter becomes extended over time. The American Arbitration Association has offices in many principal cities throughout the United States, conducts training programs for arbitrators, and offers the services of those on their panels who, by experience, have become qualified in the subject matter of a dispute. The advertising pages of the major national and regional legal newspapers contain the names and addresses of other organizations devoted to other phases of dispute resolution. A letter and resume sent to

Sydney A. Woodd-Cahusac

Finding a second career as an Episcopal priest is certainly a significant change in one's direction. The Reverend Sydney A. Woodd-Cahusac made that shift late in life and was ordained in 1986 at age 68. This came after a career with two law firms, officerships in two Fortune 500 corporations, and service as a legal officer for a research university.

Why the change? Rev. Woodd-Cahusac states that he "made this change in life focus and style so as to channel my own expanding Christian faith in a way which reaches out to others, as I believe the Christian faith requires of all, not just priests." He also believes his pro bono work over the years fits right into his present wish to be with people: talking to young people about ambitions and goals and how to achieve them, and to older people about personal and business situations.

When he pondered making this career change, he implemented it by first inquiring about the procedures involved in becoming a priest. When he approached the Bishop, Attorney Woodd-Cahusac was relieved of the obligation to attend the three years of seminary ordinarily required; but he was obliged to take the same examinations required of all candidates for ordination, to pursue the course in clinical pastoral education, and to serve in a parish (which he characterizes as something like reading for the law in a law office).

Rev. Woodd-Cahusac is emphatic in reporting that he is enjoying his career change, having found "satisfaction and meaning in my calling beyond what I had dreamed or hoped when I contemplated it, and even disappointments have had their rewards in deepening perception."

In advising others who might think about making a career change, Rev. Woodd-Cahusac cautions: Discuss obstacles and problems as well as rewards; be sure you can afford to do what you are thinking about; if you have a spouse whose life is closely bound up with yours, and who will be profoundly affected by your change, discuss it; consider whether your particular skills will be useful in the new venue; and, finally, be sure you haven't confused an avocation or hobby with a career.

these organizations will start the ball rolling toward the lawyer's new career as an arbitrator or mediator.

Many lawyers who have worked as "office types" during their careers are anxious to savor the stimulation of a courtroom atmosphere. Most bar associations are now conducting training programs for their pro bono volunteers to teach, for instance, the tax attorney the basics of handling a divorce case or the corporate lawyer about the intricacies of defending an eviction case in housing court. Those desiring to become involved in this kind of law should be confident that they will have adequate training before entering the fray.

Similarly, the many legal service organizations in cities and counties around the country have a critical need for the assistance of qualified counsel. The staff that can be assembled with the funds available to these organizations cannot cope with the number of cries for assistance they encounter every day. Much of what legal service organizations do is in the realm of litigation, and to that extent work with clients from these entities provides the retired lawyer with a new challenge: If life to date was spent as an "office" lawyer, there is now the chance to become a courtroom lawyer.

Similarly, as state and local governments struggle to balance their budgets and are faced with necessary staff reductions, the concept of using volunteers to handle some of the business of government at the state and local level is gaining popularity. Unlike service with the federal government, discussed earlier, specialized training is not a prerequisite to work at the state and local level; a person's particular experience outside government can be adapted. For example, the retired lawyer who specialized in state and local taxation may be able to volunteer services in responding to taxpayer inquiries made to state or local government headquarters; attorneys who have expertise in the drafting of construction contracts may be able to provide assistance to an overworked state, county, or municipal public works department.

For the retired attorney who would prefer to do something that is only tangentially "lawyering," there is opportunity to be of service as a mentor. A number of mentor programs are in operation, usually in connection with high schools in the community. Some have also been organized to assist prison inmates.

Dealing with people, particularly those of another generation, on a one-on-one basis and providing the benefits of a lifetime of experience can be very self-satisfying. Information on these programs is available through local bar associations and boards of education.

When considering pro bono activity, the senior lawyer needs to determine whether the work will require malpractice insurance and, if so, how that protection is to be provided. If one has retired from a corporation or law firm, one must check to see whether that entity carries any malpractice insurance that could be extended to the retiree. Should there be no such protection, there are alternatives. Legal service corporations usually carry malpractice insurance, and the volunteer lawyer providing legal services would do well to be certain that any legal work performed is under the umbrella of that policy. Work for states and municipalities can be brought within the boundaries of the malpractice policy of the state or municipality. Where feasible, the preferred course for the attorney is to consult with respect to the business, rather than the legal, aspects of proposed transactions, thereby eliminating the need for malpractice coverage. In the case of mentor programs, legal advice is not involved and there is no need for malpractice insurance.

Using Your Legal Knowledge in Law-Related Pursuits

One of your distinct advantages as a lawyer is your flexibility. There are many positions you can fill because you have legal training, knowledge, and experience.

*Law Librarianship**

Law librarianship is an attractive profession for consideration by senior lawyers seeking a second career. Law librarians are being sought after by law firms; and there are academic, government, and corporate libraries that serve lawyers, law schools, and other

*The author acknowledges with appreciation the contribution of Julius J. Marke, Esq., Professor of Law and Director of the Law Library, St. John's University, to the discussion of law librarianship. Professor Marke is also Professor of Law and Professor Emeritus of Law, New York University.

university research needs. Bar associations, government agencies, corporations, and federal, state, and local courts all have law libraries. Moreover, many firms cannot afford the services of a full-time law librarian and would find it satisfactory to have someone attend to the library on a part-time basis. If you are a lawyer who enjoys research, understands how the various legal periodical services operate, and would like to supplement your retirement income, you should investigate the possibilities in your area.

The tremendous growth of law book collections, the information explosion, the increased dependence on such technology as Lexis, Westlaw, and on-line bibliographic services, and the need to provide interdisciplinary materials in legal research, have changed the concept of the law library. It is no longer a mere collection of books in which legal authority can be found. Technological developments (computers, telecommunications, micrographics, and CD-ROM) have changed that concept to one of an information transfer network. A law librarian is now an "information specialist," and the employment outlook is favorable. Law librarians coordinate the research activities of their organizations. They suggest sources of information the lawyer can use. Even more significantly, they locate those sources when they are initially unknown to the practitioner.

Law librarians have a variety of duties and responsibilities. Among other things, they typically provide efficient specialized reference services to attorneys, paralegals, and others; they instruct and assist attorneys, paralegals, and others in legal bibliography and research; they structure and perform on-line searches of computerized bibliographic and informational databases; and provide current awareness service by previewing advance publication information, periodical literature, and new acquisitions. They may also assess the quality, depth, and scope of the existing collection; systematically tailor the acquisition of library materials; establish policies and procedures for the presentation of library materials; and prepare fiscal reports, budgets, and long-range informational plans relative to library needs.

In actual research, law librarians can find legal citations or references, suggest sources of information, verify and translate citations, assemble materials for specific projects, and prepare bibliographies. Senior lawyers, because of their long experience, generally are knowledgeable in a variety of areas; they can provide significant assistance to legal researchers because of their facility in finding the answers to questions involving business, medicine, history, the social sciences, economics, and the applied sciences.

Senior lawyers must recognize that the computer is now an essential tool in legal research; any lawyer who is not computer-literate and who espouses a second career as a law librarian must educate himself or herself in the use of the computer in legal research. A knowledge of computer science and electronic data processing is essential to law librarians and, in addition a working knowledge of one or more foreign languages, is desirable as well.

Skills in personnel management, business administration, budgeting, and public relations are often significant in the role of law librarianship.

The American Bar Association (ABA) and the Association of American Law Schools (AALS), in their law school standards for accreditation, have established criteria for qualifying law school libraries and librarians.

The ABA standards for law librarians are part of its *Standards for Approval of Law Schools* (October 1990). Standard 605 provides that: "The law library shall be administered by a full-time librarian whose principal activities are the development and maintenance of the library and the furnishing of library assistance to faculty and students, and may include teaching courses in the law school." Substandard 605(a) adds: "The law librarian should have a degree in law or library science and shall have a sound knowledge of library administration and of the particular problems of a law library." Substandard 605(b) continues: "The law library shall have a competent staff, adequate to maintain library services, under the supervision of the law librarian."

The Association of American Law Schools (AALS) applies its own accreditation standards to law schools seeking membership in the Association. The professional standards set by the AALS in its By-laws and Executive Committee regulations are more demanding than those of the ABA. AALS Regulation 8.2(a) provides that "the director of the library should have both legal and library education." AALS By-Laws 6-10 adds: "A member school shall maintain a library adequate to support and encourage the instructions and research of its faculty and students . . . a member school shall have a full-time librarian and a staff of sufficient number and with sufficient training to develop and maintain a high level of service to its program. The director of the library should be a full participating member of the faculty."

Despite these exacting requirements, many senior lawyers seeking second careers would qualify for this type of work. This is particularly true of lawyers who have had a combined business and legal career, with experience in leadership and administration.

Managers of medium-sized law firms usually are not sure when their firm needs a law librarian. Marke and Sloane, in their book entitled *Legal Search and Law Library Management* (rev. ed. 1992), estimate that the firm can afford to hire one whenever the value of the hours that the librarian saves all the lawyers in the office approximates the librarian's salary plus fringe benefits, Social Security, and related costs (see their Chapter 57, "A Guide to Hiring a Law Firm's First Librarian"). This varies from about six to ten hours a week, depending, of course, on the lawyers' average hourly rate.

They note, for example, that it will pay a twenty-five–lawyer office to hire a law librarian if the librarian saves those lawyers only fifteen minutes each for a total of six and a quarter hours a week during a forty-six–week year, when the lawyers' average rate is $135 an hour. That totals $39,531. This assures a law librarian's salary at the modest sum of $30,000, plus other costs of about one-quarter more, or a total of $37,000. Such an arrangement leaves a wide margin for profit, since the librarian can actually save lawyers between ten and twenty hours a week rather than a mere six and a quarter hours. And the time saved is usually billable time.

Aside from the profit a firm earns from a law librarian's service, the firm also obtains the added advantage of a well-developed and well-organized library, responsive to its research needs.

Around 1950, the ABA survey of the legal profession estimated that the total number of law librarians at the time amounted to about 1,600 to 1,700. Today, more than 4,700 law librarians, working in approximately 1,100 law libraries, are members of the American Association of Law Libraries (AALL).

The 4,700 members of the AALL are employed in various types of organizations that serve the legal profession. As classed by organization, they reflect the variety of opportunities that exist for senior lawyers. The types of libraries and the number of librarians are as follows:

Corporate	332
County	252
Government	515
Private firm	1,651
Independent	43
Law schools	1,416
No affiliation	367
Other	122

Lawyers seeking second careers have several different types of organizations from which to select in pursuing the possibility of a second career as a law librarian.

Law Office Administration

Similarly, there are opportunities in law office administration. The attorney who has talents in the realm of finance and accounting may learn that his abilities are in demand and salable. Likely prospects as employers are large and medium-sized firms. While many law offices employ office managers who are not lawyers, the problems faced by offices with significant numbers of lawyers—involving issues of capital provision, borrowing policy, clients who are substantial debtors to the firm, complicated tax reporting, and sophisticated employment law matters—suggest to them that a lawyer should direct their financial and administrative affairs. If you have an interest in this area, your experience may be of interest to a firm in need. A firm with this requirement may not have an attorney in-house with the necessary qualifications. Should you be willing to labor for compensation somewhat less than what you might expect from active practice, but with more regular hours and hopefully less stress, your services could be in great demand. Legal journals in your area carry advertisements for such assistance, and placement services specializing in assistance to law firms should be aware of opportunities.

9

Quasi-Legal Activities

Many lawyers would like to utilize their experience in the law and would find it difficult not to be involved with the legal fraternity. In the search for a second career, there are opportunities for such people. Two areas immediately come to mind: the whole spectrum of alternative dispute resolution and service as an expert witness.

ALTERNATIVE DISPUTE RESOLUTION*

Lawyers and other citizens have become disenchanted, to varying degrees, with our system of civil justice. First, the explosion of crime in the country, the Speedy Trial Act, and the flood of criminal defendants whose cases command priority by judges have all caused delays in disposition of civil litigation. Second, the cost of pretrial discovery, mammoth document production and endless deposition schedules, has caused a loss of faith in the system. People are searching for new ways to resolve civil conflicts; hence, alternative dispute resolution.

A few years ago, there was little choice; one could file a lawsuit or pursue arbitration. Today, the phrase "alternative dispute resolution" conjures up an entire menu of possible procedures.

Mediation is a voluntary, informal consensus-building process. A party-selected neutral mediator assists the parties in reaching a mutually acceptable agreement. Although there is an

*The author acknowledges, with thanks, the helpful assistance of Scott P. Moser, Esq., of Connecticut; Harlan Pomeroy, Esq., of the District of Columbia and Florida; and Robert Coulson, Esq., of New York, in providing data for the discussion of alternative dispute resolution.

opportunity for presentation of evidence and arguments, the mediator does not make a decision; rather, the mediator talks with the parties, usually separately on a "shuttle" basis, and attempts to bring them to a negotiated resolution. Mediation has a number of advantages. The mediator can view the dispute objectively and can assist the parties in exploring alternatives that they might not have considered on their own. The parties can generally save money through reduced legal costs and less staff time. There is less opportunity for rancor to develop between the parties, thus leaving the door open for continuance of a business relationship. And the mediator often is able to provide creative solutions or accommodations to the special needs of the parties; these can become part of the settlement.

Fact finding is either voluntary or involuntary, under Rule 706 of the Federal Rules of Evidence. A neutral third party, chosen by the parties or by the court, investigates the dispute and submits a report or testifies in court.

In a **minitrial**, the case is presented to two senior officials of each party, assisted by a neutral, third-party advisor. After the presentation, the senior officials attempt to reach a settlement. If they cannot, the advisor may render a nonbinding opinion as to the probable outcome of the case, if it were to be litigated.

Step-up negotiations is a system for attempting to solve a dispute at lower levels of two disputants, and then bringing ever-higher-ranking officers into the process. For example, a senior vice president from each company may try to resolve an issue within a specified time frame, say, two days. If they cannot, an executive vice president from each may seek a resolution in a further time of, perhaps, three days. Failing that, the chief executive officers of the companies may try for two days to reach a solution. After that time, the parties are free to pursue whatever other remedy appears appropriate.

A **summary jury trial** takes place in a courtroom before a judge or magistrate and a six-member mock jury, which may be impaneled by the court from the regular jury list. Attorneys for each side make an abbreviated presentation and the jury renders an advisory verdict. This verdict may then serve as the basis for a negotiated settlement.

Arbitration is the binding trial-like procedure with which most lawyers are familiar. There are presentations by the parties to an arbitrator or panel of arbitrators chosen either by the parties from a list supplied by a neutral organization or preselected and identified in a contract between the parties. After these presentations, which include oral testimony, exhibits, and argument, much as in a court, the arbitrator renders an award, which may be as brief as a single short sentence. No explanation of the award is required from the arbitrator or arbitrators. And there is an extremely limited right of appeal from the award.

When the American Arbitration Association is the administrator of the proceeding, upon the filing of the complaint the Association sends each party a list of fifteen or twenty names, with some biographical information. Each party strikes off the names of any person unacceptable as an arbitrator, and returns the list to the Association. The Association then appoints an arbitrator or arbitrators from the mutually acceptable names. Should all names be stricken, the Association sends out a new list; if no mutually acceptable names are selected from the second list, the Association will make an administrative appointment, but will not appoint anyone whose name was crossed off by any party.

Advantages of ADR to the Parties

The parties are in closer control of proceedings in most ADR procedures than in court litigation. They can compact prehearing and posthearing proceedings, set the schedule of events to suit their convenience, and select a neutral in whom they both have confidence. Even if the view of the neutral is unfavorable to its side, a party will give more credence to the view of a person they have helped select. As mentioned in discussing mediation, ADR processes help preserve the goodwill between the parties that is sometimes lost when disputes go to court. ADR is a private process that avoids any unfavorable publicity which may arise from court filings, which are public documents. Adverse publicity can harm a company's reputation and stimulate additional lawsuits. An adverse court decision may establish a precedent that could prove dangerous for the company. The very processes of ADR provide a climate for compromise, since they enable the parties to hear the other side's arguments and perceptions. Since ADR is voluntary, it is unlikely to be wasteful. Moreover, the ADR processes permit and encourage the greater use of the new technologies, including videotape, as well as video- and teleconferencing.

Not every dispute is appropriate for ADR. When a party wishes to delay or avoid a decision, encourage publicity, or cause high expense to an opponent, litigation may be a better route. This is certainly true when a party seeks to establish a precedent. At times it may even be less expensive to litigate, as, for example, when there is available a statute of limitations or jurisdictional defense which is certain to prevail. If evidence from uncooperative third parties is vital to a party's case, litigation may be required. And there are situations for which a judicial decision is necessary: where a public agency may be criticized if a decision is not court-mandated, where there is such bad blood between the parties that only a court directive is acceptable, or where the public interest is so great that compromise is not tolerable.

Getting Started in ADR

Many senior lawyers have had wide and in-depth experience in various types of businesses. They are well prepared to bring to the ADR processes the expertise and neutrality the parties need in order to resolve their disputes. Should you be among those who would like to become a neutral or arbitrator, there are a number of organizations you can contact to get your name on their lists. Names and addresses of these organizations are in the Appendix; among them are the American Arbitration Association, the American Stock Exchange Arbitration Department, the National Association of Securities Dealers, and the New York Stock Exchange Arbitration Department.

Getting on a list is no assurance that you will serve; you will have to be selected, based upon your experience, as being suitable for a specific case and, most importantly, acceptable to the parties.

The American Arbitration Association has more than 50,000 names on its National Panel of Arbitrators. Consequently, unless you establish a reputation as an arbitrator, the chances of being selected are somewhat similar to those of winning the lottery. By writing and speaking on a particular subject, and establishing yourself as someone with particular knowledge in a field, you increase your chances of being chosen by the Association case administrator for a panel of prospective arbitrators and accepted by the parties as a neutral.

Qualifying as an Arbitrator-Mediator

The American Arbitration Association will find you acceptable as an arbitrator or mediator if you meet the educational requirements appropriate for a particular area of expertise, you are experienced and considered to have a judicial temperament by colleagues or fellow professionals in your field, you have been active in your field for at least five years, although a minimum of eight to ten years may be required, and you are willing to volunteer some time as an arbitrator. The qualifications for service in large, complex commercial arbitrations are usually more stringent; the parties have an opportunity at the administrative conference, mentioned below, to discuss with the Association the qualifications they believe the arbitrator or arbitrators should possess.

The Association presents programs throughout the country on a regular basis to train arbitrators and mediators; you can find out when there is a program in your locality by checking with the Association's regional office in your area. A session might include a training videotape focusing on problems that could be encountered by arbitrators in actual arbitrations. Solutions are discussed and other material is disseminated. All new arbitrators are expected to attend such training sessions. Notations are made on the Association's records of new arbitrators, indicating the nature and extent of their training. Such a notation increases the likelihood that the person will be listed as a potential arbitrator. Consequently, it is advisable for an aspiring arbitrator or mediator to attend these sessions.

Compensation

An arbitrator may or may not be compensated in a given case. Generally, if the case is concluded after the first hearing day, the arbitrator's services are considered as having been provided on a volunteer basis; however, if the hearings are protracted, then the arbitrator or arbitrators are paid on a per diem basis for the days in excess of the first day.

Advantages of Service in ADR

Apart from the public service aspect of assisting in alternative dispute resolution and the personal and professional satisfaction it can bring, there are additional advantages. The work is often interesting and a challenge to our inquisitive minds. It presents an opportunity within broad limits to schedule work at times that do not interfere with other plans that retired persons usually have. Travel and other professional, business, or charitable activities are not impaired. Moreover, it presents the opportunity to be involved with other people active in the business and professional world. Importantly, it fosters an improved image of lawyers by letting it be known that lawyers can serve in healing, as well as contentious, roles and are willing to give their time freely to this end. It fulfills a need many feel to change the public perception of our profession as one of greed, arrogance, and lack of public interest.

This is not to say that working in ADR doesn't have some disadvantages. Not all arbitration work (just as not all trial work) is interesting. Some cases will be disposed of quickly; as noted previously, in arbitration, the usual practice is to require the arbitrator or arbitrators to provide the first day of hearings without compensation. In any event, work in ADR is hard work.

The ADR Agreement

When you undertake an assignment as an arbitrator or mediator, you will not operate in a vacuum. There will be a provision respecting ADR in an agreement between the parties; if that agreement was properly drawn, it will cover many details of the process. It will indicate whether pending litigation is stayed; how expenses are to be allocated; whether the decision is to be binding or nonbinding; what rules of evidence will apply; what discovery will be permitted, and whether the proceedings and discovery are to be confidential; who will be present at the ADR proceeding, and the permitted role of each person present; when and where the ADR proceeding will take place, and the schedule of presentations and of any postproceeding negotiating sessions; and whether there will be a reporter's transcription of the proceedings.

Does ADR Work?

Lawyers familiar with ADR processes can cite numerous examples to demonstrate their advantages and effectiveness. For instance, one law firm reports that ADR was used in a product liability context to effect an efficient resolution of a highly technical matter without resort to litigation. The dispute was presented to a three-member panel, including a former judge and two technical experts selected by the parties. Each was qualified in the specialty at issue in the dispute. The agreement provided that only a unanimous decision of the panel was binding. Lacking unanimity, the complainant was free, after a thirty-day cooling-off period, to commence litigation. The panel awarded $500,000 to the claimant, whose total legal fees were only $25,000.

This same firm states that it has used ADR in a variety of other matters, including three large, multimillion-dollar construction matters (settled by mediation), employment-related disputes, both plaintiffs' and defendants' personal injury cases, as well as employment termination cases.

Large, Complex Commercial Arbitrations

Within the last year or so, the American Arbitration Association has set up a series of panels of significantly experienced lawyers in each of the AAA's operating regions to serve as arbitrators in extremely large and complex cases. The Association has established guidelines to expedite such cases; the guidelines are applied whenever the disclosed claim of any party exceeds $250,000, unless there is an objection.

In large, complex cases, the Association will usually appoint a panel of three arbitrators to hear the case, although it will also honor an agreement by the parties to appoint the arbitrators.

Prior to turning over the case to the arbitrators, the Association arranges an administrative conference, conducted by its regional vice president or a staff member. At this conference, representatives of the parties discuss with the AAA questions concerning the appointment and compensation of arbitrators; the exchange of necessary information prior to the hearing; estimates for the length of hearings; commencement date for the hearings; and arrangement for hearing-room facilities.

At the preliminary conference, the parties may agree to submit their dispute to mediation to see if it can be resolved before going to arbitration. In such event, the Association will appoint as a mediator a person other than someone selected as an arbitrator. There is no additional administrative fee if the parties agree to attempt mediation.

Unlike smaller cases, where the arbitrator or arbitrators serve initially without fee, in larger, complex commercial cases the arbitrators are compensated by the parties, with payment made from deposits paid to the Association by the parties. Arrangements for such compensation are made by the Association in consultation with the parties and the arbitrators.

The Explosive Growth of ADR

One reason for the explosive growth of ADR in recent years is the concern of many lawyers that failure to advise clients of the availability of alternative processes may constitute malpractice. Robert F. Cochran, Jr., Professor of Law at Pepperdine University School of Law, argues that point persuasively in an article in the June 1993 issue of *Arbitration Journal*. Discussing the comment to Model Rule 1.2 of the ABA Model Rules of Professional Conduct, Professor Cochran says, "This comment appears to move closer to a duty to allow clients to choose ADR." He points out that in Colorado, a state rule adopted effective January 1, 1993, adds that "in a matter involving or expected to involve litigation, a lawyer should advise the client of alternative forms of dispute resolution which might reasonably be pursued to attempt to resolve the legal dispute or to reach the legal objective sought."

Even without the club of these rules, most lawyers appear to be telling clients that such things as mediation, minitrials, and arbitration are available alternatives to litigation. Many clients are electing to avoid litigation and choose an alternative. The result is an expanded opportunity for senior lawyers to participate in the process in second careers as mediators or arbitrators.

ADR is now big business. It has been reported that Judicial Arbitration & Mediation Services, Inc. (JAMS), a California-based company founded in 1979 and perhaps the largest in the industry, has gross income in the $20 million to $25 million range. The company uses retired judges only in providing dispute resolution services from branch offices strategically located in cities across the country, including New York. California judges serving the company part-time earn more than they would in California when sitting on the bench full-time. There are other companies in the field, but not all of their mediator-arbitrators are judges. Many recruit talented legal practitioners from the private bar, and thus provide an opportunity for lawyers wishing to pursue second careers.

Serving as an Expert Witness

For the lawyer seeking a second career in the law, becoming an expert witness is no different from establishing oneself in any other profession. There is the task of placing advertisements in trade journals, sending announcements to business friends and acquaintances, writing and publishing on the subject, and appearing at seminars to present papers on subjects with which you are especially familiar.

The subjects for which expertise is required are as varied as the law itself. You may be asked to offer an expert opinion on the answers to such questions as whether the details of handling of a client's case by a lawyer amounted to negligence, or whether a fee for services of an attorney was just and reasonable under all the circumstances. Perhaps you will testify as to the law of your home state where you practice and are licensed, if you are a witness in a case in a jurisdiction foreign to your home state; or you may offer an opinion as to whether a party to a merger agreement was entitled to declare the agreement terminated under certain provisions of the agreement between the parties.

Serving as an expert is not necessarily an easy task. You will have to be thoroughly familiar with the facts of the case in which your opinion is sought. If the case is one of significant size, involving many documents and a multitude of facts, you can expect to spend many hours reviewing and reading those documents. In some instances, you may have to conduct your own personal investigation of the facts, in order to come forth with an opinion that satisfies you.

You must not only be conversant with the facts of the case, but entirely current in the governing law. In all probability, it will also be necessary that you know the history of the law pertinent to your specialty and that you be conscious of its development and application to the particular set of facts involved in the case in which you will testify. You will be obliged to keep yourself current in your specialty by reading up on the latest developments and attending seminars and CLE courses dealing with the subject. Remember: If you are to be a *real* expert, you must know the law both as it was when you were a much younger lawyer and as it now is.

In addition to maintaining your competence in the area of law in which you are expert, you must also become familiar with the particular rules of confidentiality that apply to expert witnesses. Your file, including anything relevant to the opinion to which you testify in the case, will be open to opposing counsel. Consequently, you must be extremely circumspect in putting together notes and memoranda. Although the opposition's lawyer may not be able to obtain documents that reflect your thought processes, not all courts so hold; in a particular case, you will have to determine the state of the law in that jurisdiction with respect to document production by experts, and govern your conduct accordingly.

Every person who becomes a professional expert witness must be aware that every deposition, every courtroom transcript containing his or her testimony, every book and article written by the expert, will be reviewed by counsel before cross-examination. Consistency is important. Any inconsistency must be explained and have a totally rational basis. Failing that, the "expert" gets a reputation as simply a "hired gun."

Should you decide to become an expert, remember that you should not agree to testify in every case that comes along. If you are asked to testify as an expert, request an opportunity to review the file, talk to any person whose testimony will be crucial in the case, and review any critical physical evidence before you agree to take the stand. You must be convinced that your opinion is correct in the case; if you are not convinced, you will not be able to convince a judge or jury.

Serving as an expert witness provides flexibility with respect to your time. Even if your services are in great demand, you can elect to take as many cases as you can handle or as few as you wish. This sort of work is also remunerative. Expert witnesses are paid, and they generally charge on the basis of time spent in preparation for testimony. A rate commensurate with that charged when you were a legal practitioner is entirely appropriate. If you are amply paid for the hours of preparation, you may elect not to accept payment for time spent in the courtroom; you can then answer the inevitable question by stating that you have been paid for time spent in preparation but have not been paid for your testimony. Whatever the arrangement between you and your client, or your client's attorney, it is prudent and advisable to have it set out in writing. A simple letter agreement will be adequate; both the client and the client's attorney should sign that agreement.

10

Community Service to the World

Lawyers are people dedicated to the public weal. Most are extroverts and enjoy the society of others. By dint of education, they adapt to new situations and readily grasp varied concepts and ideas. Lawyers have high regard for their obligations to the community and deep sympathy for the many who are less fortunate. The few rotten apples in the barrel are indeed a tiny percentage of the lawyer population.

Lawyers across the globe consider themselves to be professionals. Although in recent years the practice of law has become more a business than a profession, attorneys—particularly, older attorneys—abhor the trend. Consequently, many are thinking that in retirement they may be able to contribute something meaningful to the world in which we live and not charge a fee in the process. There are a number of choices available for the lawyer who desires to help his fellow human beings and who is willing to volunteer his services.

Pro Bono Service

Lawyers are uniquely equipped to serve the community in a pro bono capacity; stated in plain English, this means they work for free. Those who have undertaken volunteer services without compensation almost universally report that their lives have been enriched, they have learned something new through the experience, and they recommend it to their fellow attorneys. If you are a lawyer seeking a second career, you should give serious thought to offering your talents to those who may need them the most but who cannot afford to pay you.

The opportunities for pro bono service are almost limitless. The clients you can serve are many and diverse. They are in areas of medicine (hospitals, philanthropic organizations devoted to particular diseases), assistance to particular groups with specific problems (foster care and adoption, children of single parents, the elderly, the retarded, runaway children, children of drug-addicted or HIV-infected parents, the disabled, the homeless), and the arts (museums, symphony orchestras, concert halls, botanical gardens, zoos). Then there are organizations working in the fields of special athletics for the disabled and those helping immigrants to learn our language and customs; these, too, need assistance.

Many charitable institutions lack the resources necessary to have a lawyer on staff or to pay for retained legal services. In any event, even if such funds are available, any not-for-profit institution will welcome the opportunity to save on legal expense. A retired lawyer, particularly one who is experienced as a general practitioner, will be able to contribute handsomely by volunteering his or her legal services.

Several activities of the American Bar Association are noteworthy. The ABA's Commission on Legal Problems of the Elderly has established a Volunteer Lawyers Project. Headquartered in Washington, D.C., the Project recruits volunteer lawyers and solicits financing to coordinate its training and work in pro bono service in the District of Columbia. The Dispute Resolution Section of the ABA also maintains a clearinghouse of information on how individual lawyers who wish to become involved in private or public dispute resolution can find opportunities to do so. In New York City, the Association of the Bar of the City of New York maintains a Standing Committee on Legal Assistance, which studies and advocates efforts of the profession to provide legal services to the needy. The Association publishes a volume listing those agencies providing pro bono assistance. The junior lawyers of the Association meet several times a month to discuss ways and means of providing legal assistance to those needing it; they then meet with people who need advice and provide them with counsel. The Legal Aid Society of New York and similar organizations elsewhere provide pro bono legal services to the indigent. Lawyers desiring to devote time, whether they are retired or not, will find a welcome and much information from these sources.

The organization that has taken a leading role nationally in organizing and expanding the provision of pro bono services to the poor and indigent is the National Legal Aid & Defender Association. Founded in 1911, the Association is widely recognized as the nation's premier institutional advocate for the rights of the poor and underprivileged to high-quality, effective legal assistance. In 1992 and 1993, it worked to defend federal funding and support for legal services programs, including the Legal Services Corporation. Through its project for Program Assistance and Leadership Support (PALS), it has sought to improve the quality of legal service delivered to poor and indigent clients by making the services of volunteer experts available for particular programs. In May 1993, the Association launched a new venture which it calls A Business Commitment (ABC). Working as a joint project of the Association and the ABA Section of Business Law's Pro Bono Committee, it will operate nationwide to support the work of legal services programs, community development corporations, charitable organizations, low-income housing groups, and other similar groups that cannot afford to hire lawyers. The annual budget of the National Legal Aid & Defender Association exceeds $2.2 million. These funds are provided from various sources, including grants, sales of publications, and contributions from corporations, law firms, and individuals.

Lawyers seeking a second career have an opportunity to find fields of pro bono legal service suitable to them in many geographic areas by contacting the Association, which has a national headquarters in Washington (see the Appendix).

Attorneys in New York City willing to perform pro bono legal services can obtain a free directory, *Pro Bono Opportunities: A Guide for Lawyers in New York City*, from the Robert B. McKay Community Outreach Law Program by calling (212) 382-6689. The directory provides information on eighty-seven organizations in the city, and was prepared by the Volunteers of Legal Service and the Association of the Bar of the City of New York.

In New York, information on statewide pro bono opportunities is available through the Department of Pro Bono Affairs of the New York State Bar Association, which publishes a monthly newsletter. You can reach the Department at One Elk Street, Albany, NY 12207; (518) 463-3200.

SERVING AS A LEGAL COUNSELOR TO A FOREIGN GOVERNMENT*

With the emergence of the Eastern Bloc countries into the free air of democracy, a unique opportunity has been presented to Western lawyers, and particularly to the American bar, to assist these countries in the transition from a totalitarian to a democratic legal system.

Harlan Pomeroy, who retired after a long career as a partner in Baker & Hostetler, moved to Sarasota, Florida, and prepared to settle down doing pro bono work in tutoring people seeking a high-school equivalency certificate. His wife was busy in theater work as a producer and writer. However, as Mr. Pomeroy explains, "We did feel that it would be satisfying to each of us if we could do something of a more significant and concentrated nature; perhaps we could do something in recognition of the good lives we had experienced and in particular our indebtedness to our country and the legal system underpinning our fortunate way of life."

Harlan Pomeroy then looked into a plan to go to Bulgaria for the International Executive Service Corps. This would have involved work as a volunteer for one or two months on privatization of Bulgarian state-owned industry. After delays, this plan did not go forward.

Next, Mr. Pomeroy was attracted by an article in the *American Bar Association Journal* discussing an opportunity with the Association's Central and East European Law Initiative (CEELI). He filled out an application form, was interviewed at CEELI's

---

*The author acknowledges, with appreciation, the vivid and detailed description of the work carried on in Bulgaria by Harlan Pomeroy, Esq., of Washington, D.C., and Sarasota, Florida, which he so generously provided. The discussion in this section is based on Mr. Pomeroy's contribution.

Washington, D.C., headquarters, flew back to his Sarasota home, and arranged his affairs for a year's absence. He then went through a two-day briefing in Washington, and was off to Sofia. (In the description he provided the author, he does not mention how he managed so quickly to persuade his wife to accept this revision in their plans!) In the latter half of 1993, Mr. Pomeroy completed a one-year tour in Bulgaria for CEELI. His experience provides a frame of reference for others who might choose to volunteer for similar service.

The Central and East European Law Initiative

The American Bar Association established CEELI in 1990 to assist the emerging democracies in their move to rule of law and the free enterprise system. It has placed resident liaisons and other legal specialists in Bulgaria, in other countries in central and eastern Europe, and in the states of the former Soviet Union. Thus, there are liaisons in Albania, Belarus, Bulgaria, Croatia, the Czech Republic, Estonia, Hungary, Kazakhstan, Kyrgyzstan, Latvia, Lithuania, Macedonia, Moldova, Poland, Romania, Russia/Moscow, Russia/Nizhny Novgorod, Slovakia, and Ukraine.

The CEELI volunteers are classified as liaisons (such as Mr. Pomeroy), Commercial Law liaisons, Rule of Law liaisons, and legal specialists. The legal specialists are in such areas as judicial training, criminal law, environmental law, constitutional court, finance, foreign affairs, and legislation.

Compensation

CEELI volunteers, as the name suggests, receive no compensation for their work. However, CEELI does pay certain expenses, such as transportation costs from the United States to the foreign destination and return (for the volunteer, but not for the spouse), and a reasonable allowance for rent, food, and other costs of living while in the foreign country.

The Duties of a Liaison

Mr. Pomeroy explains, "My service, as with my predecessor (who was also in Bulgaria for one year), covered most, if not all, of the functions of a CEELI resident overseas representative." His office and logistical support were provided by the Center for the Study of Democracy, a Bulgarian nonprofit organization and think tank. He also worked closely with three young Bulgarian staff lawyers. Mr. Pomeroy says that they "speak and write good English, are well-connected with key personnel in the Bulgarian government and elsewhere, and eased and facilitated both my work and my living situation immeasurably."

WORKSHOPS AND SEMINARS. Mr. Pomeroy put together a number of workshops and seminars during his stay. Among them were CEELI-organized seminars, such as the one he moderated in October 1992. This was a three-day affair dealing with the proposed copyright law. It was presented by a five-person panel, consisting of one German lawyer, one barrister from the United Kingdom teaching in the United States, two U.S. professors, and one U.S. practicing lawyer. A different high-level Bulgarian official presided over each session.

Mr. Pomeroy also ran, with a three-person panel, a day-and-a-half workshop on legal ethics for the National Bar Association of Bulgaria; in addition, a U.S. law professor conducted a discussion with Bulgarian law school representatives of law-school curricula and accreditation.

At each of these seminars and workshops, Mr. Pomeroy served as moderator, introducing the speakers and others. He also entertained the visitors and government officials and had general responsibility for the success of each project, which, he "hasten[s] to add had been conceived and planned in principle by my able predecessor."

As liaison, Mr. Pomeroy organized and moderated a series of five commercial law seminars held on successive Friday afternoons and spoke on substantive issues at two of them. The five workshop projects covered insolvency, including bankruptcy; commercial transactions; intellectual property, including copyrights and patents; privatization; and income taxation. The speakers included two Bulgarian law professors; the Ministers of Justice and Finance; the former Deputy Prime Minister; the Chief Legal Advisor to the Copyright Office, the Head of the Legal Department of the Privatization Agency; and a resident German law professor hired by the Bulgarian government to draft legislation. This series came as a result of suggestions made by the local judiciary and was reported to be a great success. It demonstrated that Bulgarians are well able to do their own continuing legal education. The language was Bulgarian, except for Mr. Pomeroy's presentation, which was in English (and interpreted by one of his colleagues).

Mr. Pomeroy also worked with CEELI to organize several workshops. CEELI supplied the text material from a workshop previously held elsewhere, which he and a German lawyer used to conduct two separate two-day workshops. These workshops dealing with international sales of goods contracts were helpful in providing practical instruction in an area of pressing current interest to Bulgarian lawyers, businessmen, and government personnel.

He also spoke at numerous seminars and workshops sponsored by others, such as the Peace Corps, U.S. Department of Commerce, and the Center for the Study of Democracy (the Bulgarian think tank, and Mr. Pomeroy's host in Bulgaria). Among the subjects on the programs were privatization, insolvency, copyright, the Bulgarian legislative process, and international trade.

ANALYSIS OF PROPOSED BILLS. Another of the projects undertaken by the CEELI liaison, either individually or in conjunction with a group of lawyers assembled by CEELI, was the analysis of proposed bills. Mr. Pomeroy made the analysis himself in the cases of draft bills on taxation and bankruptcy. CEELI's other experts assisted when the bills involved such topics as special investigative means; information law; explosive substances, weapons, and ammunition; and waste management.

CONCEPT PAPERS. Shortly before Mr. Pomeroy's arrival, CEELI had been requested to prepare and deliver to him (for hand delivery to the requesting government officials) general discussions by ABA volunteers, selected for their expertise, of alternative approaches the Bulgarian government might take in drafting legislation on five different subjects: securities regulation, regulation of merchants (consumer protection), currency exchange controls (including money laundering), investment funds, and government procurement.

In commenting on the effect of these documents, Mr. Pomeroy says,

> Generally, these papers would discuss the approaches taken on the particular subject by a number of different countries so that the bill drafters would have the benefit of current and diverse thinking on the particular subject. I would hand deliver these to the requesting government officials with an offer of further assistance. Usually this would result in something else we were requested to do for them. We tried to pursue the ensuing legislative drafting, which for internal political reasons was generally not open to scrutiny until a draft bill evolved and was ready for consideration by the Council of Ministers or its drafting arm, the Council on Normative Acts.
>
> We have been told that these Concept Papers have been immensely helpful in the initial drafting stage of proposed legislation.

LEGISLATIVE DRAFTING. As Harlan Pomeroy explains,

> Initially, I did very little actual drafting. However, as time went on and I became involved with more projects and more persons, I found myself assisting with the actual redrafting of legislation, as with the first part of the proposed individual income tax bill, working with a United States Treasury aide assigned to the Ministry of Finance, and a Bulgarian tax expert.

Anyone interested in designing legislation and preparing draft bills would find an outlet for this interest in joining a CEELI project.

ARTICLES. Writing also occupied much of Mr. Pomeroy's time. Two significant articles were prepared by him and published (500 copies of each) in the "Issues in Bulgarian Law" series initiated by his predecessor. Mr. Pomeroy's articles are entitled "The Privatization Process in Bulgaria," a 47-page article published in April 1993, and "Bulgarian Government Structure and Operation—An Overview, Including the Constitution, Legislature, Executive, Judiciary and Local Self-Government," a 44-page document published in August 1993. These publications were designed not only for English-speaking Westerners, but also for the many Bulgarians who both speak and read English. Through their wide distribution, they have attracted the attention of government officials, lawyers, judges, and law school faculty and students to the CEELI program and the presence of its liaison in Bulgaria.

"SISTER" LAW SCHOOL PROGRAM. While in Bulgaria, Harlan Pomeroy interviewed Bulgarian law professors interested in going to the United States to study and/or teach at an assigned American law school enrolled under the program. Thus, Mr. Pomeroy had access to law faculties in Bulgaria, an opportunity to observe them in action, and to work with their members on various projects.

WORK WITH THE LAW SCHOOLS. There was an opportunity to confer with faculty members, work with them on administrative matters from time to time, and address the law students themselves, including a matriculating new class. He was able, as he says, "to gain valuable insight into the workings of legal education in Bulgaria."

WORK WITH INDIVIDUALS AND OTHER INSTITUTIONS. As CEELI liaison, Harlan Pomeroy would meet with various persons to discuss problems they were encountering in seeking to develop a project or to gain action on a privatization matter. Through these meetings, he learned the status and problems with commercial activity in Bulgaria, while the conferees were assisted in thinking through the problems they faced and arriving at their possible solutions.

A Unique Experience

CEELI and Peace Corps volunteers typically serve one term, which is one year for CEELI liaisons and two years for Peace Corps business volunteers. After their terms, these people return to their private lives in the United States. Mr. Pomeroy notes:

> It is not surprising to find in these volunteers a dedication and commitment often not discernible in other Westerners and for many of whom a tour of duty in a particular country such as Bulgaria is just another assignment on the way to another more coveted post or perhaps to retirement.

More than in private practice and in the private business sector, the liaison, or at least this liaison, was exposed to Americans, with the U.S. Embassy and sponsored by some American sources (some even were volunteers), who seemed untutored in the basic civilities of professional life; some of them lacked important social graces, making my work as liaison more difficult and less pleasant than it should have been.

This attitude shows—and the persons with whom we work in the host country do not take long to figure out—these differences in attitude on our parts. Notable exceptions were the Ambassador, the Deputy Chief of Mission (until September 1993), and a few others. It is understood that in this respect the U.S. Embassy in Bulgaria was not typical of U.S. embassies generally; it was certainly not typical of other Western embassies in Sofia, either.

Further, a sense of humor on the part of the liaison is very useful in lubricating the machinery for the process in which we are jointly engaged.

I enjoyed a particular sense of camaraderie in my work with volunteer members of the Peace Corps and individuals sponsored by the United States Treasury and Justice Departments (generally persons who elected to come to Bulgaria). And, of course, with my three young Bulgarian colleagues at the Center for the Study of Democracy with whom I worked on a daily basis, there is a special bond.

At the farewell reception given for us, attended by more than 100 friends and officials, the former Bulgarian Deputy Prime Minister, in his formal remarks, said that the CEELI program in his country the past two years had been the most effective source of Western assistance.

Family Life

Mr. Pomeroy tells us that, if one is married, a CEELI assignment without an accompanying spouse can be difficult. There is a limited number of expatriates in each CEELI state, and as he has explained, these people often have different attitudes and approaches to living abroad. In Bulgaria, the accommodations for the liaison are relatively pleasant and comfortable. The Pomeroys found shopping in the open markets a challenge, especially in winter when vegetables and fruit were scarce.

During their one-year stint in Bulgaria, the Pomeroys were visited on separate occasions by each of their three children and by other family members and friends. Thus, the educational experience of the CEELI stint was extended to another generation.

Lawyers thinking of following the example of Harlan Pomeroy and applying for a CEELI assignment should draw the attention of their spouses to the work of Mrs. Pomeroy while in Bulgaria. She joined the staff of the local affiliate of The Voice of America. This is the independent Bulgarian station, Radio Vitosha.

Five mornings a week, Mrs. Pomeroy broadcast the Bulgarian news in English. Her newsmagazine program, which she called "Sofia Brief," was a collection of folklore and human-interest stories and interviews with prominent Bulgarians. Barbara Pomeroy wrote and narrated these features, which were aired twice daily. She also wrote "What's On in Sofia," a guide to cultural events in the city, which she broadcast on Saturday and Sunday mornings. Mrs. Pomeroy's work opened up new vistas both to Harlan and herself. As Mr. Pomeroy observes, "It was a public service not only to Westerners, but also to many Bulgarians who liked to practice their English by listening to her programs."

Any lawyer in search of a second career abroad, and blessed with a spouse having some of the talent of a Barbara Pomeroy, will find great opportunity in serving as a CEELI liaison. The emerging democracies of the former Soviet Union are in desperate need of accurate reports of *real* life in the United States and other Western countries, rather than the distorted view presented by Hollywood productions. American lawyers and their spouses who are good communicators can fill that need.

Advantages of Serving as a CEELI Liaison

From the sketch of the various and varied activities of Harlan Pomeroy in Bulgaria, it is evident that there is a wide range of opportunity available to an imaginative individual taking on a CEELI assignment, limited only by such constraints as are imposed by the CEELI mandate and the Agency for International Development grant, which supports CEELI in part.

Mr. Pomeroy has listed some of the advantages he sees, based on his experience as a CEELI liaison:

- Challenging, varied work, supported by the individual lawyer's education and legal experience and by CEELI itself
- Living and working abroad and getting to know another people and their culture well
- An opportunity to make a contribution to the difficult and very critical transition from Communist totalitaliarism to the rule of law and the free enterprise system
- Learning, and helping to mold, a new system of government and a new body of law, and its likely impact on, and harmony with, European civil law
- Making friends in another country, many of whom will be friends for life
- Assisting able young foreigners to go to the United States for training and to see what our country (with its often similar problems) is like
- Traveling in the host country and in neighboring countries

Disadvantages of Serving as a CEELI Liaison

Accepting an assignment overseas as a CEELI liaison is not for everyone. There are disadvantages, and these must be considered and weighed against the advantages before one makes a decision to apply.

Although there is only a one-year commitment, this is a long time for some to be away from family and friends. Communication with the United States is not easy. There is a seven-hour differential between eastern Europe and the East Coast of the United States, and there is, of course, the matter of expense and difficulty in getting a phone call through to the United States.

Language can be a substantial barrier. The Pomeroys had to contend with the Cyrillic alphabet and the Bulgarian language, both difficult. They did not deem it practical to devote to learning the language the time and energy otherwise available for substantive work, particularly in light of their relatively short stay in the country. Nonetheless, both were able to pick up some of the language in the course of their visit.

In most CEELI countries, the American community is not large. And Americans who reside there often have different agendas and philosophies as to why they are in the host country, and have different attitudes toward it and its residents.

People with medical problems need to pay particular attention to the resources that will be available to them, since many of the former Soviet Bloc countries have limited medical facilities. Also, housing, food, and the general amenities of living are in short supply.

Americans are accustomed to getting things done expeditiously, and the seeming slow pace of reform in the Eastern Bloc countries can at times be frustrating.

Summing Up

Harlan Pomeroy's experience in Bulgaria is probably typical of what a retired lawyer, seeking a second career, may gain from a CEELI assignment. He says that some things which many perceive as disadvantages were not viewed by him or his wife as disadvantages. He explains:

> My wife and I can think of few more rewarding and emotionally satisfying ways to spend a year in the continuing retirement process. Perhaps we were lucky, and I am sure we were in many respects (such as being assigned to Bulgaria), but we helped create some of our "luck."
>
> For a reasonably positive person with a normal energy level, in good health, an ability to get along with and to be sensitive to the outlook of others, and with the twin senses of adventure and humor, this experience is great.

So if you are thinking of an interesting way to live and work abroad in retirement, you might consider applying for a CEELI assignment.

Nonlegal Services

Lawyers need not think that volunteer activity must necessarily relate solely to the law. The broad knowledge and wide range of abilities possessed by most attorneys make them valuable to institutions in a variety of activities.

The many organizations in New York City that search for volunteer assistance are examples of the types of opportunities open throughout the country. Perhaps the greatest need is in the health care area. Agencies such as the American Cancer Society and the Lighthouse for the Blind use volunteers in a variety of activities. Hospitals—Beekman Downtown Hospital, Bellevue Hospital Center, Harlem Hospital, Long Island College Hospital, Memorial Sloan-Kettering Cancer Center, New York Hospital, and St. Vincent's Hospital and Medical Center—all need volunteers to assist with patients and nonpatients alike.

Many organizations dedicated to assisting children are in need of volunteer assistance, and most of these assignments require no legal training. The Angel Guardian Home, Big Brothers of New York City, Boy Scouts of America, the Brooklyn Children's Museum, the Cooke Foundation for Special Education, Covenant House, East Harlem Tutorial Program, Girl Scout Council, Hale House Center, the Starlight Foundation, and Volunteer Services for Children all need help. Some volunteers assist in administrative functions, while others have direct contact with the clients of these organizations. The work may involve the care and feeding of infants and very young children, supervision of play of older children, and tutorial assignments for underachieving and retarded children.

Some of the assignments in the health care area and in assistance to children may be stressful and depressing, particularly to anyone who is facing difficult times in his or her own life. However, there are other opportunities to volunteer in activities that will offer refreshing moments, and perhaps a mental challenge. The American Museum of Natural History, Asia Society, Bronx Zoo, Brooklyn Museum, Carnegie Hall, New York Botanical Gardens, New York City Ballet, New York City Opera, and New York Philharmonic are examples of entities that can use your assistance in clerical work, in running gift shops, and in serving as tour guides.

Not every community has as many places where one can volunteer, but most communities have some organizations akin to those mentioned above. I recently had the opportunity to visit St. Patrick's Cathedral in New York and had a pleasant conversation with a security guard (it is a sad commentary on our times that churches must employ security guards). This gentleman, seventy-five years of age, had retired and was living in a very comfortable home on Long Island. But he was lonesome and took the position at St. Patrick's to be able to mingle with people, have a sense of doing something worthwhile, and supplement his income, all at the same time. If you do some investigation, you will be able to uncover a second career for yourself that meets whatever criteria you have established.

People who have spent their entire lives in business or in the law often have a hankering to teach. The spread of mentor programs in our inner cities has provided an opportunity for many to indulge this ambition. For example, the Senior Lawyers Committee of the Association of the Bar of the City of New York established a mentor program for young people in the Martin Luther King High School who aspired to attend law school. Retired lawyers gave a few hours of their time on a regular basis to help inform these potential attorneys as to what would be required of them and what they might hope to reap from their efforts. The East Harlem Tutorial Program provides one-on-one tutorial assistance to junior high-school students in the East Harlem area. The International Center, another New York City–based entity, offers one-on-one tutoring for foreign members of the Center in conversational English. For those whose interest is in athletics, the Manhattan Special Olympics Program provides a chance to assist the mentally handicapped; the program includes a variety of sports.

Nearly every community in the country has a branch of the American Red Cross. Throughout the year, but especially in times of a major catastrophe, the Red Cross needs volunteers to assist in its relief efforts. *Greenwich Time*, the local paper in my hometown, carried the story of Yvette Montoura, a retired New York City school teacher who became a member of our local chapter, where she took the course in disaster response. When the Great Flood of 1993 struck the Midwest, Yvette went to a shelter in Iowa that was home to scores of flood refugees, including more than thirty children. When their parents went to work—which they still had to do, despite being displaced from their homes—the retired teacher took over. She reported that 80 percent of the volunteers helping out were retirees from all walks of life: "We had retired bankers, college professors, cops, you name it." Retired senior lawyers, especially those wanting to do something apart from the law, may find that becoming a Red Cross volunteer will be a satisfying experience.

In this book, we have offered suggestions on a variety of second careers available to those in the legal profession, both the enchanted and the disenchanted, young and old, who have reached a moment of decision. Consider the advantages and disadvantages, the pluses and minuses, of each—including the alternative of maintaining your present course. Then decide whether or not you have reached a turning point.

APPENDIX

Places to Start

The following list of names and addresses of persons and organizations is not offered as a complete or comprehensive list. Rather, it presents a sampling of representative organizations with whom one may communicate in search of a second-career opportunity.

For example, the American Arbitration Association has regional offices throughout the United States. Lawyers seeking to become arbitrators or mediators might well get in touch with the nearest regional office of the Association; those addresses are available from the Association's New York headquarters.

For Service as an Administrative Law Judge

Office of Personnel Management (OPM)
Office of Administrative Law Judges
Career Entry Group
Room 2433
19 E Street NW
Washington, DC 20415

For more information, write to:

Chief Administrative Law Judge
Office of Hearings and Appeals
One Skyline Towers
5107 Leesburg Pike
Falls Church, VA 22041;

Ask for: "How to Become an Administrative Law Judge"

For Alternate Dispute Resolution Opportunities

Alternate Dispute Resolution Subcommittee
Howard I. Aibel, Esq., Chair
Senior Lawyers Committee
Association of the Bar of the City of New York

42 West 44th Street
New York, NY 10035
212/258-1000

American Arbitration Association
140 West 51st Street
New York, NY 10020-1203
212/484-4000

American Stock Exchange Arbitration Department
86 Trinity Place
New York, NY 10006
212/306-1427

Council of Better Business Bureaus
4200 Wilson Blvd.
Arlington, VA 22203
703/276-0100
(or contact your local Better Business Bureau to volunteer)

Dispute Resolution Program Director
ABA Dispute Resolution Section
1800 M Street NW
Washington, DC 20036
202/331-2200

Mediation, Inc.
P.O. Box 16205
Chapel Hill, NC 27516

National Association of Securities Dealers
33 Whitehall Street
New York, NY 10004
212/858-4000

National Institute for Dispute Resolution
1901 L Street NW
Washington, DC 20036
202/466-4764

New York Stock Exchange Arbitration Department
20 Broad Street
New York, NY 10005
212/656-2772

Pre-Suit Mediation Program
International Association of Defense Counsel
20 North Wacker Drive
Chicago, IL 60606
312/368-1494

United States Arbitration and Mediation, Inc.
6000 Westland Building
100 South King Street
Seattle, WA 98104

(Addresses of other offices throughout the United States can be obtained from this Seattle headquarters.)

Other Opportunities

Bet Tzedek House of Justice
145 S. Fairfax Avenue
Los Angeles, CA 90048
213/939-0506

Board of Examiners
U.S. Department of State
Washington, DC 20521

Business Volunteers for the Arts
130 East 40th Street
New York, NY 10016
212/819-9277

Central and East European Law Initiative (CEELI)
Attention: Mr. Mark S. Ellis, Executive Director
American Bar Association
Suite 200, South Lobby
1800 M Street NW
Washington, DC 20036-5886
202/862-8533

Citizens Democracy Corps
2021 K Street NW
Washington, DC 20006
202/872-0933

City of Los Angeles
Office of Public Counsel
3535 West 6th Street
Los Angeles, CA 90005
213/385-2977

Commission on Legal Problems of the Elderly
Attention: Ms. Nancy Coleman
American Bar Association
1800 M Street NW
Washington, DC 20036
202/331-2630

Connecticut Legal Services, Inc.
425 Main Street
Middletown, CT 06457
203/344-0447

Constitutional Rights Foundation
407 South Dearborn Street
Chicago, IL 60605
312/663-9057

Corporation Counsel's Office, Law Dept.
City of New York
Attention: Linda G. Howard, Esq.
Administrative Asst. Corporation Counsel
100 Church Street
New York, NY 10007
212/788-1100

Education for Democracy/U.S.A. Inc.
P.O. Box 40514
Mobile, AL 36640-0514

The Foundation Center
Attention: Ms. Sara Engelhart, President
79 Fifth Avenue
New York, NY 10003
212/620-4230

Georgia Legal Services
10 Whitaker Street
Savannah, GA 31401
706/651-2180

Habitat for Humanity International, Inc.
Habitat and Rhuch Streets
Americus, GA 31709
912/924-6935

Harriett Buhai Center for Family Law
4315 Leimert Blvd.
Los Angeles, CA 90008
213/298-1443

Institute for Educational Leadership, Inc.
Attention: Mr. Michael D. Usdan, President
1001 Connecticut Avenue NW
Washington, DC 20036
202/822-8405

International Association of Justice Volunteerism
University of Wisconsin Criminal Justice Institute
P.O. Box 786
Milwaukee, WI 53201
414/229-5630

International Executive Service Corps
Attention: Mr. Jeffrey Lockhard
333 Ludlow Street
Stamford, CT 06902
203/967-6000

Lawyers Committee for Human Rights
330 Seventh Avenue
New York, NY 10001
212/629-6170

LCE Volunteer Lawyers Project
AARP
601 E Street NW, Bldg. A, 4th Fl.
Washington, DC 20049
202/434-2271

Legal Aid Society of Metropolitan Denver
1905 Sherman Street
Denver, CO 80203
303/837-1313

Legal Center for Non-Profit Organizations, Inc.
Manuel Schultz, Esq.
Timothy Lyman, Esq.
P.O. Box 693
New Haven, CT 06508-0693
203/624-5415

Legal Services of Eastern Missouri, Inc.
625 North Euclid Avenue
St. Louis, MO 63108
314/367-1700

Legal Counsel for the Elderly
601 E Street NW
Washington, DC 20049
202/434-2120

Legal Services of Middle Tennessee, Inc.
211 Union Street
Nashville, TN 37201
615/244-6610

Mayor's Office of Public–Private Partnership Programs
253 Broadway
New York, NY 10007
212/240-4300

McKay COLP (Robert B. McKay Community Outreach
Law Program)
Special Panel of Volunteer Lawyers
Office of the Executive Secretary
c/o Association of the Bar of the City of New York
42 West 44th Street
New York, NY 10036
212/382-6689

Mental Health Advocacy Services
1336 Wilshire Blvd.
Los Angeles, CA 90017
213/484-1623

Mentor Program, Senior Lawyers Committee
Attention: Robert Layton, Esq., Chair
Association of the Bar of the City of New York
42 West 44th Street
New York, NY 10036
212/754-2700

National Endowment for Democracy
Attention: President
1101 15th Street NW
Washington, DC 20005
202/293-9072

National Legal Aid & Defender Association
1625 K Street NW
Washington, DC 20006-1604
202/452-0620

National Park Service
Office of the Volunteer Coordinator
U.S. Department of the Interior
1849 C Street NW
Washington, DC 20242
202/208-3100

National Volunteer Center
111 North 19th Street
Arlington, VA 22209
703/276-0542

New York Cares
140 East 58th Street
New York, NY 10022
212/753-6670

Partnership for the Homeless, Inc.
110 West 32nd Street
New York, NY 10001
212/947-3444

Retired Senior Volunteers Program
ACTION
1100 Vermont Ave. NW
Washington, DC 20525
202/606-4855

(ACTION sponsors many different programs using senior citizens as volunteers.)

Retirement Options, Inc.
Attention: Mr. Donald L. Praeger, Chairman
645 Madison Avenue
New York, NY 10022
212/644-4998

Southern Ohio Legal Services
1212 Sycamore Street
Cincinnati, OH 45210
513/241-6284

State Bar of California
Office of Legal Services
555 Franklin Street
San Francisco, CA 94102
415/561-8267

Toledo Legal Aid Society
Senior Legal Services Program
1 Stranahan Square
Toledo, OH 43604
419/321-1578

United Nations Education, Scientific and Cultural Organization
Attention: Director
United Nations Plaza
New York, NY 10071
212/963-5995

Utah Legal Services, Inc.
124 S. 400 East
Salt Lake City, UT 84111
801/328-8891

Volunteer Lawyers for the Arts
1 East 53d Street
New York, NY 10022
212/319-2787

Volunteers of Legal Service
Attention: Wm. J. Dean, Executive Director
17 Varick Street
New York, NY 10013-2476
212/966-4400

For Assistance in Career Determination

Ms. Belinda C. Plutz
Career Mentors, Inc.
15 West 26th Street
New York, NY 10010
212/725-1076

ABOUT THE AUTHOR

George H. Cain has been a lawyer for more than forty-five years. During this time, he served as a director and corporate officer of several listed corporations, as well as their general counsel. In more recent years, he practiced law as a partner in Day, Berry & Howard, a major New England law firm, concentrating in corporate law and business litigation. He retired in 1990 and became Of Counsel to the firm. A graduate of Georgetown University and Harvard Law School, he served as an Air Force officer in both World War II and the Korean War. Mr. Cain continues to be active in a number of professional organizations, including the Senior Lawyers Division of the American Bar Association, where he is a member of the Council, the Division's governing body. He has written extensively for legal publications, and frequently lectures, on a variety of subjects. His biography appears in *Who's Who in America*. Mr. Cain lives in Connecticut with his wife, the former Constance Sullivan Collins. He has four sons by a previous marriage, a stepson, and three stepdaughters, all of whom are grown and launched on their own careers.

INDEX